Red Wing
ART POTTERY

IDENTIFICATION
& VALUE
GUIDE

Red Wing
POTTERY
HAND PAINTED

B. L. DOLLEN

COLLECTOR BOOKS
A Division of Schroeder Publishing Co., Inc.

The current values in this book should be used only as a guide. They are not intended to set prices, which vary from one section of the country to another. Auction prices as well as dealer prices vary greatly and are affected by condition as well as demand. Neither the Author nor the Publisher assumes responsibility for any losses that might be incurred as a result of consulting this guide.

Searching For A Publisher?

We are always looking for knowledgeable people considered to be experts within their fields. If you feel that there is a real need for a book on your collectible subject and have a large comprehensive collection, contact Collector Books.

On the Cover:

Top: Vase #1162 - 9", gloss pea green/gray, vine handled vase, $32.00 – 40.00.
Center left: Plate, orange fleck, bottom marked "Red Wing," 10" hearthstone dinner plate, $5.00 – 8.00.
Center right: Vase #E12 - 7", semi-matte turquoise, grooved RumRill bowl, $48.00 – 54.00.
Bottom left: Vase #1356 - 7½", semi-matte green/white snail shaped vase, $24.00 – 30.00.
Bottom right: Planter #259 - 6", semi-matte pink, swan planter, $42.00 – 48.00.
Back cover: Deer Inset #531 - 10", ivory/brown wipe, large deer insert frog, $38.00 – 50.00; Bowl #5261 - 12", ivory/brown wipe, Renaissance centerpiece bowl, $45.00 – 60.00.

Cover design by Beth Summers
Book design by Terri Stalions

Printed in the U.S.A. by Image Graphics

Contents

Red Wing
POTTERY

HAND PAINTED

Dedication

This book is dedicated to all the people who are Red Wing collectors and to those who will join us in the future. It is a passion that, as we know, gives us great joy. It is the thrill of the hunt, the joy of the find.

Acknowledgments

I wish to express my appreciation for the help I received in researching Red Wing art pottery at the Goodhue County Historical Society Library, located in Red Wing, Minnesota.

The librarians were very pleasant and helpful. Reference materials used were:
Copies of original Red Wing Catalogs dated 1930s through 1965. Held by the Goodhue County Historical Society, in Red Wing, Minnesota.
Also knowledge gained from a tour of the Red Wing Art Pottery on display at the Goodhue County Historical Society, Red Wing, Minnesota.

Special Acknowledgment

I would like to give a special thank you to my husband Roger, for driving me many miles in search of information for this book, and last but not least, for taking up the slack at home while I was writing.

Photographs by Troy A. Petry

Pricing & Value Guide

The prices included in this book are not meant to set prices. They are a general guide on the pricing which can vary considerably due to demand and the area where the item is purchased. The price ranges in this book are an average of prices in different areas of the country. The prices given assume that the pottery is in very good condition. Cracks or chips take away from the value of art pottery. In turn, perfect pieces command higher prices.

You may find some bargain prices at yard sales, auctions, and thrift stores. However people at thrift stores and auctions are now more knowledgeable about antiques and you will find most of them separate the antiques and sell them at considerably higher prices than their other items.

You will also find some areas where the prices are considerably higher. This is the result of several different factors. But as a general guide for pricing you will find these to be in the range of most Red Wing art pottery you will find.

Red Wing
POTTERY
HAND PAINTED

Red Wing Fever... It has taken the country by surprise. When the art pottery line was originally introduced by Red Wing in the early 1930s, it was a way for the company to diversify and also give consumers a line of vases and other items to use in their homes. Today it is one of the most sought after collectibles in the art pottery field. For years, many people enjoyed collecting the Stoneware Line of Red Wing and as they collected the values grew. Now the art pottery has come into its own and is finding a place in the history of collectibles.

It started with me because of one planter left to me by my late mother. It was a matte white with a green interior and fancy flower handles. You could tell by looking at it that it was a quality item of that era. I loved that planter, not only because it belonged to my mother, but also because it looked great anywhere I put it. I had determined by this time that it was Red Wing.

I had the planter for several years, when one day while looking in an antiques store, I saw a vase that caught my eye. It was the same colors and style as my favorite Red Wing. In checking, I found it indeed was a Red Wing, so I purchased the vase to go with the planter I had. Well, it was not long, before I was looking for Red Wing everywhere we went and purchasing my finds. Suddenly I was hooked... and my collection grew.

While I was collecting, I looked for a book to help guide me in my purchases. I could not find a book on the art pottery. So, a few months back, I decided to do some research and write a book on Red Wing art pottery for my own knowledge on the values, age, and perhaps names of some of the lines of art ware and to help others who, like me, get a great deal of pleasure from collecting Red Wing. From what I understand, there are a great number of us in the U.S. who have Red Wing fever.

There is something about articles from the past that create a certain ambiance wherever they are placed. They have a certain style that is never outdated, it is only enhanced by time. Their value also increases with age, as people learn to appreciate their quality and style.

If you have a collection, check out your pieces. If you do not have any Red Wing, look around and find a piece you like, buy it and check the book to see if you have perhaps found an unusual piece or a bargain. Whatever you get, will be sure to add beauty and style to any setting, and chances are good, that you too could catch Red Wing fever. Enjoy.

History of Red Wing

In 1861 a German immigrant, Joseph Pohl, settled on a farm near Red Wing. He soon discovered that the clays near the farm were excellent for making utilitarian wares such as crocks and churns. He started making these stoneware items in an old school house and sold them to the local citizens. Mr. Pole left the area around the time of the Civil War, but he is credited with discovering the clay around Red Wing.

In 1868 David Hallem began operating a stoneware pottery in his home in Red Wing. This venture was not successful and was eventually purchased by a group of citizens who formed a corporation under the name of Red Wing Stoneware Company. Mr. Hallem was the first to supervise this operation in 1878. The venture proved successful and Red Wing Stoneware Company was recognized as one of the leading producers of stoneware in the United States.

Soon two competitors entered the field, Minnesota Stoneware Company in 1883, and Northstar in 1892. After four years the Northstar Company closed. In the early 1900s both Red Wing Stoneware Company and Minnesota Stoneware Company burned. After constructing new plants the two companies merged forming the Red Wing Union Stoneware Company. They later introduced a pottery line in addition to the stoneware line. Eventually the company created an art ware line. The Brushware Line was the first decorative art ware introduced in the late 1920s. In 1930 they introduced the art pottery lines with fine smooth glazes and classical shapes.

The name of the pottery was changed in 1936 from Red Wing Union Stoneware Company to Red Wing Potteries, Inc. That same year they also contracted to produce a line of art pottery for a marketing agent in Little Rock, Arkansas, named George Rumrill. Mr. Rumrill designed a lot of the items in this line and it was named RumRill after him. They continued to produce RumRill until 1938 when George Rumrill ceased purchasing from Red Wing. Mr. Rumrill then contracted with other potteries.

Red Wing discontinued the stoneware line in 1947, and continued to produce the art pottery lines until 1967 when labor problems and a dwindling market forced them to close their doors. Red Wing Pottery had been producing their wares for 89 years when they closed.

The remaining stock was sold piece by piece at a salesroom across the street from the pottery. A legend in their field, Red Wing Pottery, will never be forgotten.

1878 . . . . . . Red Wing Union Stoneware Company

1883 . . . . . . Minnesota Stoneware Company (competitor)

1892 . . . . . . Northstar Company (competitor)

1896 . . . . . . Northstar Company went out of business

1900 . . . . . . Minnesota Stoneware Co. burns (spring)

1900 . . . . . . Red Wing Union Stoneware burns (fall)
              (both companies rebuild and merge)

1908 . . . . . . Red Wing Union Stoneware Company
              (official reincorporating)
              (Trademark RED WING)

1929 . . . . . . Introduced Art Ware Line

1930 . . . . . . Introduced Fine Art Pottery Line

1935 . . . . . . Introduced Dinnerware Line

1936 . . . . . . Red Wing Potteries (legal name change)

1947 . . . . . . Ceased Production of Stoneware

1967 . . . . . . Plant Closed

Learning About Red Wing Pottery

The art pottery line of Red Wing was first introduced in the 1920s with the Brushware Line. The pottery was a crude line using the same clay they used to make the Stoneware Line, with some modifications.

In the late 1930s, due to a decrease in the market for the Stoneware Line and because they were running out of the local clay they used, they hired Belle Kogan, a New York designer, to design a line of fine art pottery. Art pottery by definition, is any article created by a gifted artist, for beauty rather than utility, and could encompass even tableware. This line required blended earthen clays, which they imported from other states. The pottery had fine smooth glazes and classical forms. The lines were very ornate, each having distinctive handles and base decorations that matched their names. There is a list and description following this chapter. These first lines either Red Wing or RumRill are very hard to find.

The glazes on the art ware were soft velvety matte, semi-matte, and gloss in an array of colors. One of the most popular lines is the soft ivory matte with purplish brown sprayed on, and then wiped off, leaving color in the recesses. Belle Kogan created these lines, among them are the Renaissance, Magnolia, and the Vintage Lines. This method was used on raised designs of fruits and flowers on vases, bowls, and other items.

IVORY WITH BROWN WIPE METHOD. These pieces are an example of the ivory with brown wipe lines. Note the dark coloring in the recesses.

They later simplified and standardized the early lines, which were carried on throughout the 1950s and 1960s. Eva Zeisel, another New York designer, created other art ware and the Town and Country Dinnerware Line introduced in 1946.

Glazes

One of the most attractive aspects of the art ware was their use of different color glazes to decorate a single article. One shade was used on the outside and it was lined with a different color, such as white with green, pink with white, blue with pink, and others.

MULTICOLORED AND PLAIN GLAZES. These pieces are an example of the color glazes. The multicolored glazes came in many different two-tone colors. The plain colors were more limited. There is a list of the different colors following each chapter.

TYPES OF GLAZE FINISH. These pieces show the different types of glazes used over the years. There was matte, shown on the green mandarin bowl; semi matte, shown on the white and green snifter vase; and gloss, shown on the yellow and brown snail-shaped vase.

Bottom Markings

All the art ware made by Red Wing was numbered and marked Red Wing on the bottom of each piece. The marks were of several varieties, but all said Red Wing in them. The earlier Brushware Line had an ink stamp marking. One stamp was a circle with the wording "Red Wing Union Stoneware, Red Wing Minn." Another stamp said "Red Wing Art Pottery" with no circle. The bottom markings on the later art ware were inscribed by hand.

These are a few of the bottom markings. Note the numbers on the later art ware.

BRUSHWARE. This is the bottom marking on a Brushware vase. Notice that there is no numbering on this.

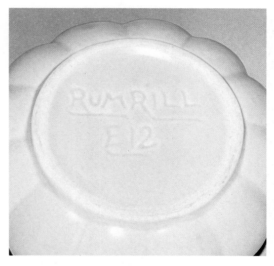

RUMRILL. This is the bottom marking on a RumRill bowl. The numbering system on the RumRill was done starting with lower numbers.

RED WING, 1940s. This is the bottom markings on a 1940s' vintage Red Wing vase.

RED WING PITCHER. This is the bottom marking on a small Red Wing pitcher. Notice there was no numbering on this. It was probably part of the Dinnerware Line and they were not numbered.

RumRill

There was one exception to the Red Wing markings, this was due to the fact that in the late 1930s Red Wing contracted to produce a line of art ware for George Rumrill. All of the art ware produced for him, was marked RumRill on the bottom. The RumRill pieces were also numbered. George Rumrill created many of his own designs, but some of his articles were made from the Red Wing molds. Therefore, you can find some pieces of both potters that are identical except for the bottom markings. George Rumrill ceased purchasing his wares from Red Wing in 1938.

RumRill. This group shows a few of the RumRill line. Note the similar color glaze style in the two-tone colors that Red Wing used.

Some of the Red Wing art ware also had a paper wing label placed on it. It is not known what the selection method was for doing this, but articles that are found with the label in tact are worth up to $10.00 more in value, depending on the item and the condition of the label. The wing labels came in gold or silver with a red wing and red lettering saying Red Wing. There was also a smaller label in a different wing shape. This label was red with silver markings on it. Some special edition labels have been found. One such label is gold with a red wing on it and writing depicting the 75th anniversary of Red Wing. The inscription reads "75th Year, Red Wing, 1878 – 1953."

Wing Labels

SILVER WING LABEL. This is an example of the silver wing label. Notice that it reads "Red Wing Art Pottery."

GOLD WING LABEL. This is a gold label with identical markings as the silver label. The only difference is the gold color. The labels were placed randomly on the pieces of pottery. Some were even placed sideways.

ANNIVERSARY WING LABEL. This is one of the special wing labels done in gold and red. Notice the writing depicting their 75th anniversary.

RED WING LABEL. This is an example of the different red label. This was probably the original label used in the 1930s and later changed to the bigger silver and gold label. You do not find many pieces with this label on them.

Bottom Numbers

Red Wing produced a catalog of their wares for wholesale and retail businesses. The early catalogs were numbered on the front. Later in the 1950s and 1960s they had spring and fall catalogs, that referred to which edition they were on the front of the catalog. The number markings on the bottom of the art ware was the production and also catalog number of that particular item. The numbers started with the first lines of art pottery in the 1930s and 1940s, starting with the 100 series. This number stayed with the piece throughout the life of production on that particular piece. Some of the pieces were produced from the beginning in the 1930s on through the 1960s. In the 1950s and 1960s the numbering system went up through the 5000 series. However, at no time did Red Wing use all the numbers in a given series. Some of the numbers have a letter preceding them, such as B1409. It is known that Belle Kogan put a B in front of the numbers on some of the articles she designed. It is known that designer Charles Murphy also added the initial M in front of the numbers. Red Wing also would add or drop a color of a line from the spring to fall catalog. In doing so, they may have been limiting the number of a certain colored piece. All colors were not always available. The art ware was sold differently at given times. An item may have been available to purchase individually in one catalog and by the dozen in another.

The following pieces show examples of some of the different numbers that are found on the bottom of Red Wing art ware.

PLAIN NUMBERS. These pieces show an example of how numbers only were used on some items.

LETTER AND NUMBER. These pieces show an example of how the designer placed an initial before the number. The B is for Belle Kogan and the M is for Charles Murphy. Also notice the different ways they put Red Wing USA in the bottom markings.

It is relatively easy to recognize a piece of Red Wing by sight, once you are familiar with the semi matte, two-tone coloring, or some of the other gloss colors. Then you can identify the piece by looking at the bottom markings.

These pieces give an overall view of some of the Red Wing art ware to be found.

ART POTTERY 1930 – 1960. These pieces range from the first art pottery of the 1930s through the 1960s.

Early Art Pottery Lines

1930s

FLUTED GROUP

Biblically shaped articles with contoured outsides and handles that were part squared and part rounded.

GRECIAN GROUP

Greek-style articles with smooth outsides and handles that were joined to make a circle from top to bottom or snake shaped.

SHELL GROUP

Shell-shaped articles very fancy articles each containing one or more shell shapes and no handles.

SYLVAN GROUP

Victorian-style articles, very ornate with raised flowers and fluted edges.

SWAN GROUP

Articles that were either shaped as a swan or had swan head and neck handles.

CONTINENTAL GROUP

Ornate European-style articles with raised flowers on the outside and fancy flowered handles.

TRUMPET FLOWER GROUP

Smooth-lined articles decorated with either a trumpet flower or trumpet flower handles.

FLORENTINE GROUP

Smooth-lined articles decorated with a flower and all different style handles.

INDIAN GROUP

Classic Indian style articles with no decorations.

FERN GROUP

Fluted articles decorated with a fern leaf and no handles.

CLASSIC GROUP

Grooved articles with large raised bumps on the outside and geometrical shaped handles.

MANDARIN GROUP

Greek-style articles with smooth outsides shaped in octagon and rectangular pieces.

MANHATTAN GROUP

Art deco style with smooth lines and no handles.

RENAISSANCE GROUP

Fluted articles decorated with long leaves and no handles.

VINTAGE GROUP

Fluted articles decorated with grapes either on the item or as handles.

NEO-CLASSIC GROUP

Smooth-lined articles decorated with marble-like balls for handles.

Art Pottery – 1920s & 1930s

The Brushware Line of art pottery was introduced by Red Wing in the late 1920s. The line consisted of jardinieres, urns, vases, and bowls. There were also water pitchers and glasses to match. The Brushware Line came in three colors, walnut green, cobalt blue, and tan with dark brown glaze inside. The designs were acorns, cattails, flowers, and leaves. There was also a Greek design in this line.

The fine art pottery was produced starting in the early 1930s. The earlier lines, listed after chapter one, are quite rare and very hard to find. Their value is hard to determine because they are not often found for sale. There were also some plainer lines produced in this period. Some of which can be found on the following pages. The colors on the early lines were mostly limited to white, white and green, pink, blue, pink and white, and green. They were all done in a matte or semi-matte finish.

This group of pottery shows an overall view of what to look for in the art pottery that was produced first.

EARLY LINES OVER-ALL VIEW. From left to right: In back SWAN LINE Planter; BRUSH-WARE LINE Vase; MEDALLION LINE Magnolia Vase. In Front RUMRILL Bowl.

17

Brushware Line

The Brushware Line while crude holds a special place in the history of the art pottery lines and in the hearts of the collectors. The line is the beginning of a pottery legend. Being the oldest line of art pottery, Brushware is harder to find and commands higher prices than the later pieces. Its look really fits the category of antique.

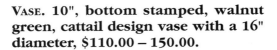

VASE. 10", bottom stamped, walnut green, cattail design vase with a 16" diameter, $110.00 – 150.00.

You can tell by looking at the Brushware pieces, that they were made from the same crude clay as the stoneware. The color was wiped on the outside of the clay giving a tan and green or blue look to the item. The color on the inside was done in a semi-matte glaze and often spilled over the edge of the pottery and was fired on there.

VASE. 8", bottom stamped, cobalt blue, cattail design vase with a 12½" diameter, $90.00 – 110.00. The cobalt blue Brushware is harder to find than the green and often has a higher price. This piece is from the collection of Bernice Ehlers, Shelby, IA.

Bowl. 6", bottom stamped, walnut green, Greek design bowl, $65.00 – 90.00. The larger 10" bottom stamped, Greek design bowl is known to run $120.00 – 150.00.

Urn. 7", bottom stamped, walnut green, flower design urn, $90.00 – 120.00. Note the spill over of the green glaze used on the inside. This urn has a different bottom stamp. It reads "Red Wing Art Pottery."

JARDINIERE. 9", bottom stamped, walnut green, leaf design jardiniere with a 10" diameter, $90.00 – 130.00.

JARDINIERE. 5", bottom stamped, tan/cocoa brown, Greek-type design with a 7" diameter, $50.00 – 85.00. The finish on this jardiniere gives the look and feel of sand. Notice the character between the pillars. It is the picture of a woman, but it is often mistaken for a Monk.

WATER GLASS. 4¾", no bottom stamp, walnut green, Greek-type design water glass, $22.00 – 28.00. Notice this design is similar to the jardiniere above. The pillars are the same with a different character in between. This glass is part of a water pitcher and glasses set. The sets run $320.00 – 400.00. Most of these sets were not bottom stamped.

Medallion Line

The Medallion Line produced in the late 1930s consisted of several groups. Among these are the Magnolia, Vintage, and Renaissance Groups. These groups were all made with the ivory and colored wipe finish in a semi-matte glaze. They were decorated with flowers and grapes. Some of the flower groups were called English Garden, Magnolia, and Cherry Blossom. The grapes were the Vintage Group. This line came in a variety of vases, bowls, and candleholders. There were also some accessory pieces made. The Medallion Line was one of the most popular lines that Red Wing produced.

MAGNOLIA GROUP

The Magnolia Group was the best selling of Red Wing's art pottery. This group was done in the ivory wipe method and decorated with large magnolia flowers. It came in two wipe colors brown and green. However, the green is quite hard to find. You will most often see the brown color. The group consisted of many different vases, bowls, and candleholders. There was also a small box with a lid and an ashtray made in the Magnolia. You will notice that it is one of the loveliest groups of art pottery.

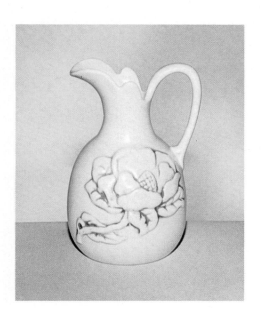

VASE. #1012 - 7", ivory/brown wipe, handled Magnolia pitcher vase, $28.00 – 40.00.

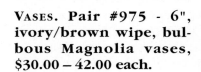

VASES. Pair #975 - 6", ivory/brown wipe, bulbous Magnolia vases, $30.00 – 42.00 each.

VASE. #1213 - 9", ivory/brown wipe, tapered Magnolia vase, $42.00 – 55.00.

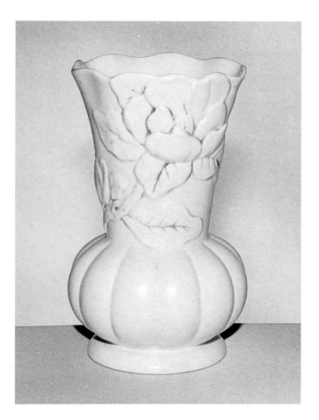

VASE. #1030 - 9", ivory/brown wipe, large Magnolia vase, $46.00 – 58.00. This vase shows the full view of the magnolia flower used on these pieces. It is interesting how they used different shaped flowers to fit the pottery, depending on the size and shape of the item.

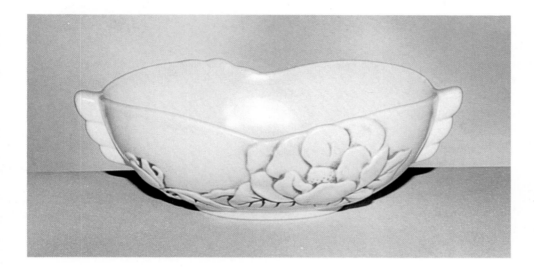

BOWL. #1016 - 10½", ivory/brown wipe, oblong, wing handled Magnolia bowl, $38.00 – 46.00. There was also a 12½" bowl like this one.

BOWL. #1223 - 12½", ivory/brown wipe, oblong Magnolia bowl, $48.00 – 56.00. Notice that this bowl has a very heavy wipe. On some items the brown wipe is hardly visible. This bowl and the previous one were also part of a console set with candleholders.

CANDLEHOLDERS. Pair #1029 - 7½", Magnolia candleholders, $36.00 – 42.00 each. These candleholders were quite expensive when originally sold in the 1930s. Selling for $24.00 a pair. Note the silver wing label on each candleholder. They were also used as part of a console set.

ASHTRAY. #1019 - 4½", ivory/brown wipe, Magnolia ashtray, $25.00 – 32.00. This is one of the accessory pieces of the Magnolia Group. Made so that you could have all matching pieces of a decor. There was also a small covered box 4 x 3½" in this group. You do not often see these two items for sale.

CONSOLE SET. #1223 - 12½" bowl, **#1029 - 7½"** candleholders, ivory/brown wipe, Magnolia console set, $120.00 – 150.00. A console set was also pictured with these candleholders and the large wing handled bowl in an original Red Wing catalog.

RENAISSANCE GROUP

The Renaissance Group was also a popular line of pottery for Red Wing. Part of the Medallion Line, it consisted of vases, bowls, candleholders, and a centerpiece set. They were all quite ornate, done in the ivory wipe method and decorated with fancy style leaves. The centerpiece set consisted of a bowl and a frog insert that was a deer figurine. This set has come to be known as the Red Wing Stag. The deer centerpiece and the candleholders are the items most often seen. The vases and bowls are not often found.

DEER INSET. #531 - 10", ivory/brown wipe, large deer insert frog, $38.00 – 50.00. Notice the holes in the base of the deer stand. These are for flowers. The insert was put into the bowl with water and the flowers placed through the holes in the insert. These inserts, whatever shape, are called frogs.

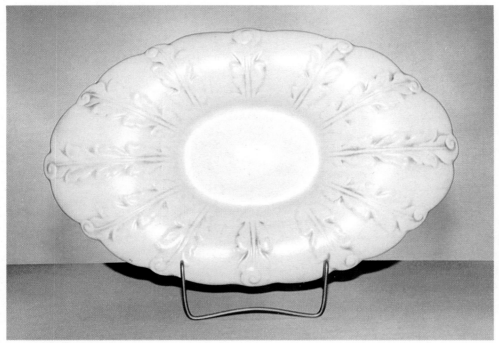

BOWL. #526 - 12", ivory/brown wipe, Renaissance centerpiece bowl, $45.00 – 60.00.

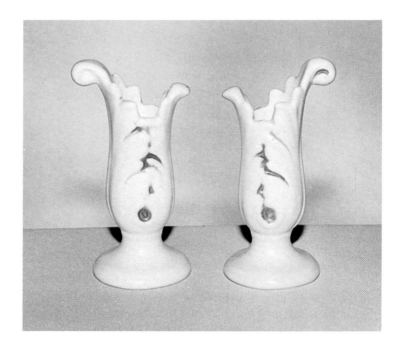

CANDLEHOLDERS. #529 - 6", ivory/brown wipe, Renaissance candleholders, $20.00 – 28.00 each. Notice some of the Red Wing candleholders looked more like small vases.

CENTERPIECE SET. #526 - 12" bowl, #531 - 10" insert, #529 - 6" candleholders, ivory/brown wipe, Renaissance centerpiece set, $145.00 – 160.00. Centerpiece without candleholders, $98.00 – 120.00. The bowl and deer insert are known to have been produced in the 1950s in the zephyr pink fleck. That color seems to command higher prices.

ENGLISH GARDEN GROUP

The English Garden Group was also part of the Medallion Line. It consisted of vases, bowls that were a similar shape to the Magnolia bowls pictured, and candleholders. As with the rest of the Medallion Line this group was done in the ivory wipe, using brown, turquoise, or yellow wipe, in a semi-matte glaze. The pieces had very unique ornate shapes and were very attractive. In any color the English Garden pieces are quite hard to find.

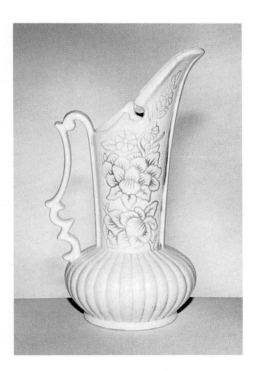

**VASE. #1187 - 12½",
ivory/brown wipe, English
Garden pitcher vase, $55.00 –
85.00. Notice the ornate handle on this vase.**

**CANDLEHOLDER. #1190 - 6",
ivory/brown wipe, English
Garden candleholder, $22.00
– 28.00 each.**

Miscellaneous Groups

These groups were not known to be part of any particular Red Wing line. However they are some of the first art pottery produced by Red Wing. Sold under group names, they are part of the early line items listed after Chapter I. The following groups are some of the plainer groups of the early art pottery and although scarce, can be found.

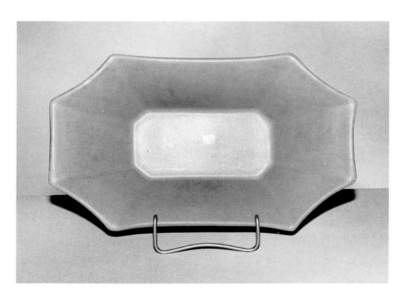

MANDARIN GROUP

This group came in a variety of vases and bowls, all have an octagon shape resembling a Greek style. The grouping appears to be some the earliest art ware done, because of its matte glaze. It is hard to know the colors of this group, since they are seldom seen anywhere.

BOWL. #331 - 11", matte green, Mandarin bowl, $46.00 – 52.00. This piece had the heavy matte of the first art pottery.

INDIAN GROUP

The Indian Group came in a variety of vases, bowls, candleholders, and pitchers done in a semi-matte of bright colors. They were bulbous items and appeared to made more for use, rather than decoration.

PITCHER. #50 - 8", semi-matte orange, Indian pitcher, $38.00 – 46.00. The inside was simply glazed stoneware. It originally came with a pottery and cork stopper not shown in this picture. The pricing given is for a pitcher with stopper.

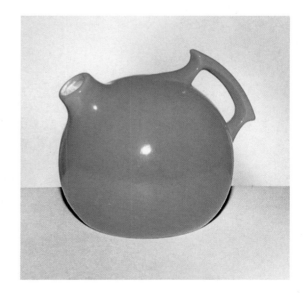

SYLVAN GROUP

The Sylvan Group consisted of very ornate vases, bowls, and candleholders. The candleholders being the plainest of the items, the vases and bowls were very decorative with fluted tops and fancy handles. They were made in the semi-matte ivory and brown wipe and decorated with leaves and flowers. Any other colors are hard to determine, since this group is rarely seen.

CANDLEHOLDERS. Pair #397 - 5½", ivory/brown wipe, Sylvan candleholders, $22.00 – 28.00 each.

CLASSIC GROUP

The Classic Group consisted of vases, bowls, and candleholders. There was also a jar type vase with a lid and a basket bowl. They were done in a semi-matte glaze. Some of colors known are pink/white and white. The items all had a grooved appearance and fluted tops.

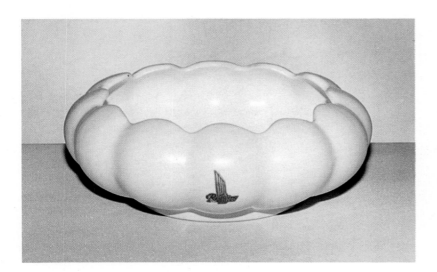

BOWL. #279 - 9", semi-matte pink/white, silver wing label, Classic bowl, $48.00 – 56.00. The pink colored art pottery seems to command a higher price than the others. Note the silver wing label.

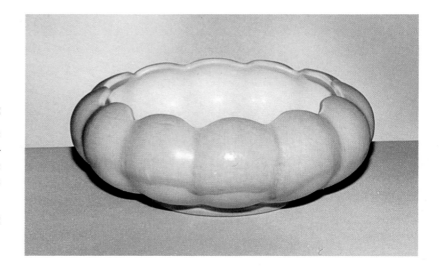

BOWL. #278 - 9", semi-matte green/white, Classic bowl, $38.00 – 46.00. Notice how the green glaze has run on this bowl. It almost seems to be matte glaze that fired odd.

SWAN GROUP

The Swan Group consisted of vases, bowls, planters, and urns decorated with swans, either as a handle or the body of the item. The colors known are plain pink and plain white done in a semi-matte glaze.

PLANTER. #259 - 6", semi-matte pink, Swan planter, $42.00 – 48.00. This piece has a very heavy glaze on it, almost resembling a matte glaze.

VINTAGE GROUP

The Vintage Group was produced in a variety of vases, bowls, compotes, and candleholders. The pieces were decorated in the ivory and brown wipe. They were produced in large sizes ranging from 9½" to 15", except the candleholders. The pieces were very ornate, some of the bowls were shaped as baskets with grape vine handles. You will not see a lot of this group for sale.

URN. #616 - 11", semi-matte ivory/brown wipe, pitcher urn, $75.00 – 110.00. Notice the heavy brown wipe which makes the grapes appear as a cluster.

CANDLEHOLDERS. Pair #622 - 5½", semi-matte ivory/brown wipe, grape cluster candleholders, $32.00 – 46.00 pair. Notice the grape leaf along with the cluster which adds detail.

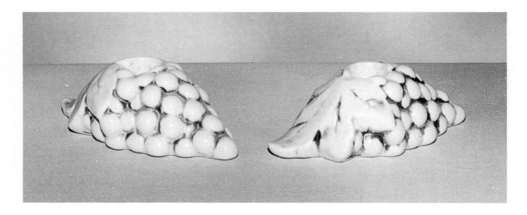

MISCELLANEOUS GROUP

Red Wing always had a miscellaneous group in their catalogs. They consisted of vases, bowls, candleholders, and planters. Some of the items resembled the named groups and sometimes there would be items that could be used with some of the named group items, such as flower frogs. The following are two vases in the miscellaneous group of the late 1930s.

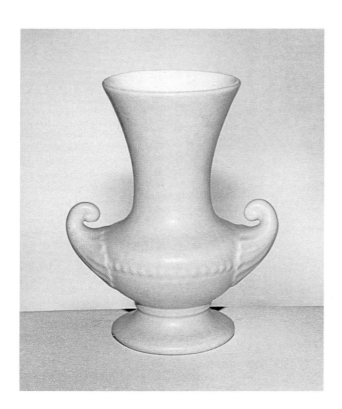

VASE. #504 - 7½", turquoise matte/white, miscellaneous vase, $42.00 – 50.00. This vase is very similar to a vase in the miscellaneous Mandarin Group.

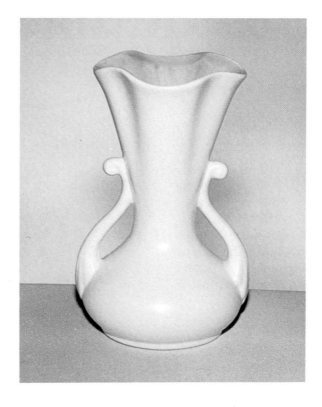

Vase. #505 - 7½", semi-matte white/green, miscellaneous vase, $30.00 – 36.00. This vase is also very similar to one in the Mandarin miscellaneous group, only that one was 9½".

RumRill Line

The RumRill Line was made for a potter named George Rumrill who contracted Red Wing to make his pottery from 1936 to 1938. It was bottom marked RumRill and numbered. The numbers however, were started in the single digits, unlike Red Wing pottery which started in a higher series. The RumRill numbers were often preceded by a letter like the Red Wing pottery. The line consisted of various vases, bowls, candleholders, swans, and other items. Quite a few of the RumRill pieces look identical to some of the Red Wing items. This is due to the fact that some of the same molds were used for both lines. The RumRill pottery is harder to find than Red Wing, due to the short period it was produced at Red Wing. Therefore, it usually commands a higher price than its Red Wing counterpart. The identical pieces also carried the same numbers on the bottom. The only difference was the pottery marking, Red Wing or RumRill.

George Rumrill continued to produce his pottery at other potteries after he left Red Wing. The pieces produced somewhere other than Red Wing are also marked RumRill. However, those pieces also have "Made in the USA" in the bottom marking. None of the items produced at the Red Wing Pottery contains those words.

VASE. #J10 & H10 - 9½", semi-matte pink, handled RumRill vase, $55.00 – 75.00. This vase has an unusual double number marking. Perhaps two designers worked on this vase and both put their initial on the bottom marking.

VASE. #K8 - 12", semi-matte white, horn of plenty RumRill vase, $40.00 – 46.00.

VASE. #394 - 9", semi-matte turquoise/white, genie-type Rum-Rill vase, $48.00 – 56.00. The glaze on this piece is almost a matte and it is identical to the miscellaneous Mandarin vase of Red Wing's pictured previously.

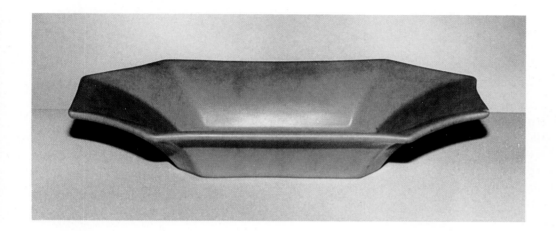

BOWL. #331 - 12", matte green, Mandarin-type bowl, $52.00 – 65.00. This bowl is also identical to a Red Wing piece.

BOWL. #276 - 6", semi-matte eggshell/turquoise, grooved RumRill bowl, $40.00 – 44.00. This bowl is identical to a bowl in the Red Wing Classic Line except for color.

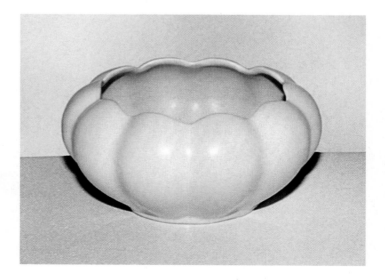

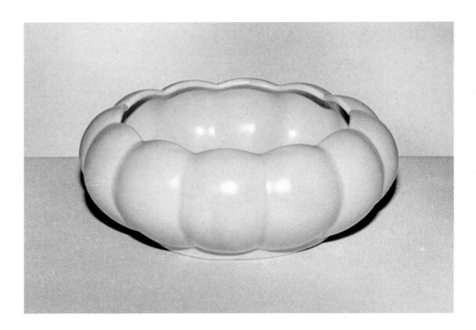

BOWL. #E12 - 7", semi matte turquoise, grooved RumRill bowl, $48.00 – 54.00. This bowl is an example of the quality work done at the Red Wing Pottery. Notice the perfect color and glaze on this piece.

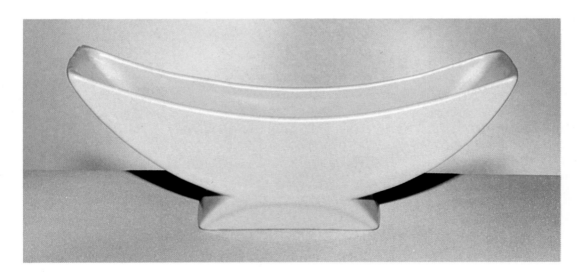

BOWL. #H18 - 11½", semi matte pink, boat-shaped bowl, $30.00 – 36.00.

PLANTER. **#259 - 6"**, semi-matte white, RumRill Swan planter, $42.00 – 55.00. Notice the partial RumRill stamp on this item. Although not intact, it shows that stamps were added to some of the RumRill pieces.

PITCHER. **#50 - 8"**, gypsy orange, RumRill pitcher, $56.00 – 62.00. Identical to the Red Wing Indian Group pitcher. This piece has an unusual bottom stamp marking instead of the indented markings usually found on the Red Wing and RumRill pieces. The stamp reads RumRill in blue ink.

Color Chart

1920s & 1930s

Brushware	Walnut Green
	Cobalt Blue
	Tan/Cocoa Brown
Medallion Line	Ivory/Brown Wipe
	Ivory/Green Wipe
RumRill	Pink
	Matte White
	Gypsy Orange
	Turquoise
	Eggshell
	Yellow
	Ocean Green – Green Lined
	Seafoam Ivory – Nile Green Lined
	Dutch Blue – White Stripes
	Crocus Green Gray – Pink Lined
Other Red Wing	Matte White
	Blue
	Pink
	Green
	Yellow
	Green – White Lined
	Matte White – Green Lined
	Pink – White Lined

Note: Although this does not include all the colors of this vintage, it gives a good overview of them.

Art Pottery - 1940s

The art pottery of the 1940s was very similar to the simpler pottery of the 1930s. During this period Red Wing was starting the process of making their art pottery pieces a lot less ornate, without the fancy decorations added in the 1920s and 1930s. This was done not only to cut the cost and offer a more affordable line of pottery, but was also a means of having a more marketable product. People felt they could use the vases, bowls, and other items for everyday use, and did.

They still included some of their earlier pieces in their catalogs, such as the Magnolia, Vintage, and Renaissance groups which were a part of the early 1940s vintage. Later in the 1940s the pottery was mostly offered in miscellaneous groups with no line names, this practice carried on through the 1950s. They did however, always have a least one decorator line.

The items made were vases, bowls, compotes, and cornucopias. There were also candleholders, planters, and console sets. They were done in a variety of plain and two tone colors, in a semi-matte glaze.

OVERALL VIEW 1940s POTTERY. The pieces found most often of this period will be done in white/green with a variation of green colors. You will also find pink/white, green/white, and some plain white.

Vases

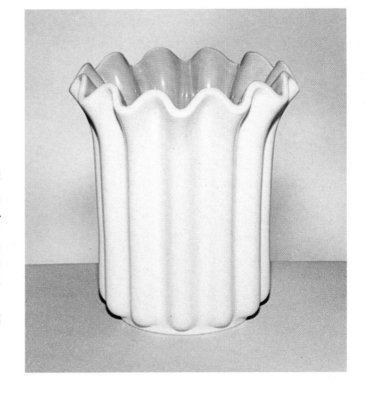

VASE. #1169 - 7½", semi-matte white/green, ribbon vase, $36.00 – 42.00. This vase was also made in 8½" and 9½" sizes. It is one of the items which continued on through the 1950s and 1960s, having the same bottom number, only done in different colors.

VASE. #946 - 6", semi-matte white, fan-shaped small vase, $20.00 – 26.00.

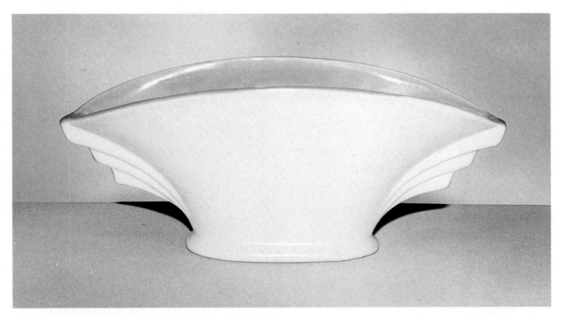

VASE. #None - 12", semi-matte white/green, fan-type vase, $32.00 – 38.00. This vase is unusual with no bottom number. The bottom marking simply reads Red Wing. Perhaps it is a sample item, although sample items have been found marked as such with "Sample" placed on the bottom. It is identical to a vase in the earlier Manhattan Group, #537 - 12". However with no bottom number, it can not be identified as such.

VASE. #892 - 7½", semi-matte white/green, fan vase, $32.00 – 42.00. This piece was also produced on through the 1950s and 1960s.

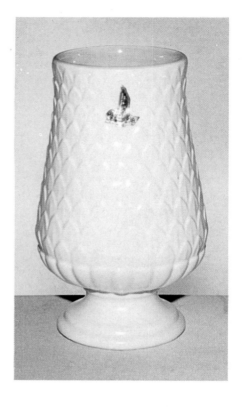

VASE. #M1442 - 8½", semi-matte white/green, snifter vase, $38.00 – 46.00. Also produced in the 1950s and 1960s. Note the silver wing stamp.

VASE. #1170 - 6¾", semi-matte white/green, sawtooth vase, $36.00 – 42.00. Also produced in the 1950s and 1960s.

VASE. #871 - 7½", semi-matte white/green, trophy vase, $36.00 – 42.00. Produced through the 1950s and 1960s in a variety of colors. It was also done in zephyr pink fleck, which commands a higher price.

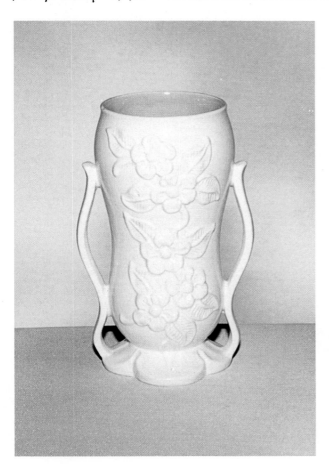

VASE. #1360 - 7½", semi-matte white/green, flower-embossed vase, $32.00 – 44.00.

VASE. #1360 - 7½", semi-matte green/white, flower-embossed vase, $28.00 – 34.00. Identical to the last vase except for color, this picture is the back side of the vases.

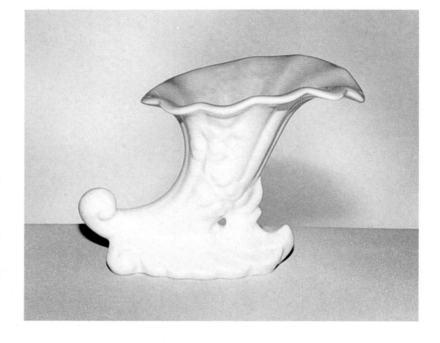

VASE. #1097 - 5¾", semi-matte white/green, ivy-decorated cornucopia vase, $32.00 – 38.00.

VASE. #1356 - 7½", semi-matte green/white, snail-shaped vase, $24.00 – 30.00. Notice how the outside glaze, which looks almost like a matte, has fired through to the inside white making spots of green on the inside of the vase.

By now you have noticed the many different shades of green used with the white combination. This was due to the fact that the paint was hand mixed for color, so the green was different in each production run. However the pieces they ran with a given batch of paint would be the same green inside. On the next batch of paint the pieces of the run would all be a different shade than the previous batch.

While collecting you will find several pieces with the same green inside. It would seem that the production runs were quite large. Perhaps making all of a season's items at one time. The other colors on the pottery pieces were not so noticeably different.

The next two pottery pieces were done in the pink/white combination. The shade of pink is a little different on each vase. The pink color is not seen as often as some of the other colors, and usually sells for a higher price, especially the pale pink color on the ribbon vase. It is quite a lovely piece.

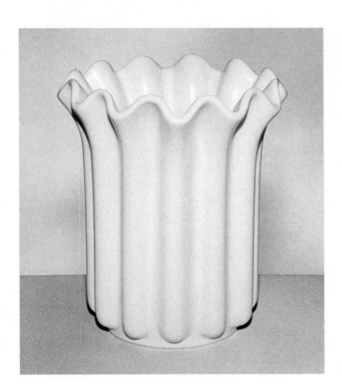

VASE. #1169 - 7½", semi-matte pink/white, ribbon vase, $38.00 – 42.00. The pale pink glaze looks almost like a matte. This vase is identical to the one pictured earlier, except for color.

VASE. #1202 - 10½", pink/white, leaf motif vase, $30.00 – 36.00. This vase has the look of some of the earlier pieces.

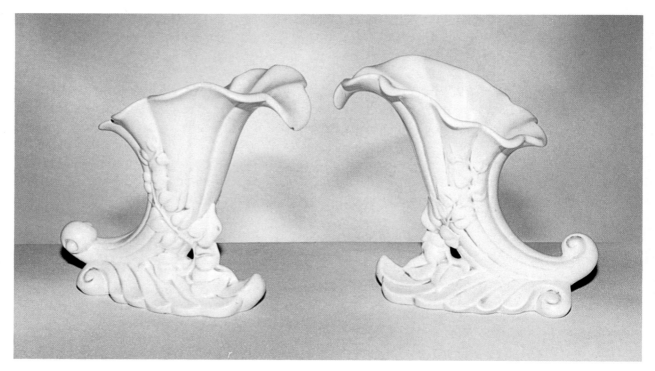

VASES. Pair #1098 - 8½", semi-matte ivory/brown wipe, cornucopia vases, $34.00 – 42.00 each. These vases decorated in ivy, are part of the Medallion Line produced in the 1930s with production carried on through the 1940s.

Bowls

BOWL. #1322 - 5½", ivory/brown wipe, Magnolia bowl, $30.00 – 36.00. This bowl was also produced in the 1930s Medallion Line.

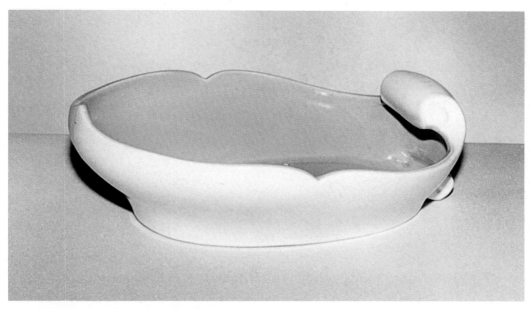

BOWL. #1092 - 10½", semi-matte white/green, garden club-style bowl, $26.00 – 34.00. The style of this bowl is very similar to a group of bowls produced in the 1960s, called garden club bowls. They will be pictured in a later chapter.

BOWL. #M1447 - 12½", semi-matte white, contoured bowl, $20.00 – 26.00.

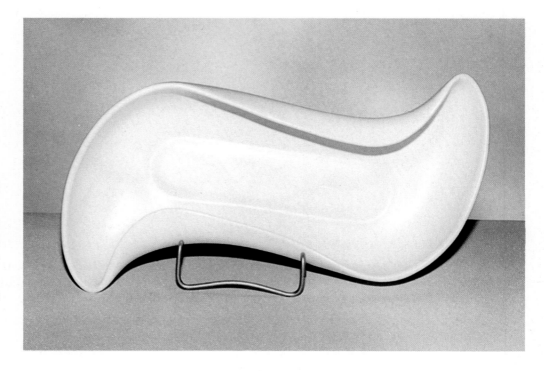

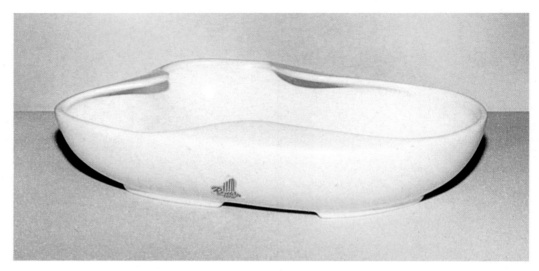

BOWL. #899 - 6½", semi-matte white, small footed bowl, silver wing label, $20.00 – 24.00. Although this piece has a wing label on it, the stamp is in quite bad shape and does not add to the value of the bowl.

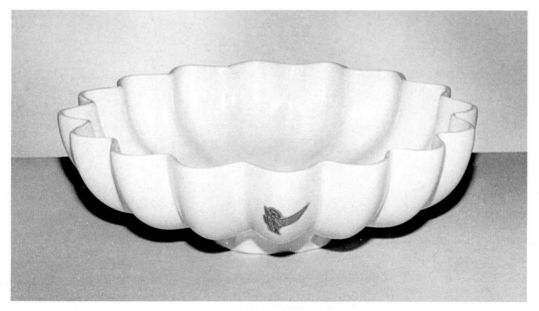

BOWL. #1620 - 10", semi-matte white, silver wing label, scallop edged console bowl, $36.00 – 42.00. Notice the perfect wing label on this piece. This bowl was also part of a console set which had matching candleholders.

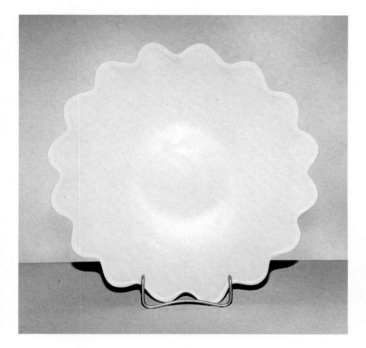

BOWL. #426 - 10¾", semi-matte green/white, scallop-edge flat bowl, $26.00 – 32.00. Shown above is the inside of this bowl, and below is the outside. This was a particularly flat piece of pottery, which limited it uses.

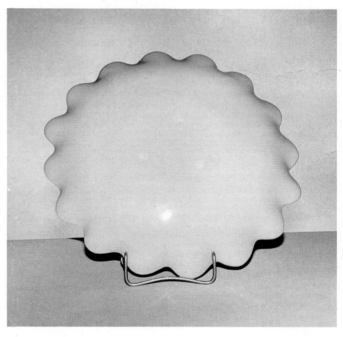

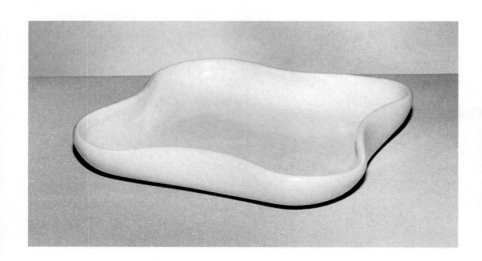

BOWL. #1037 - 7½", semi-matte pink, square bowl, $24.00 – 28.00. The color is the same pale pink as the ribbon vase pictured earlier.

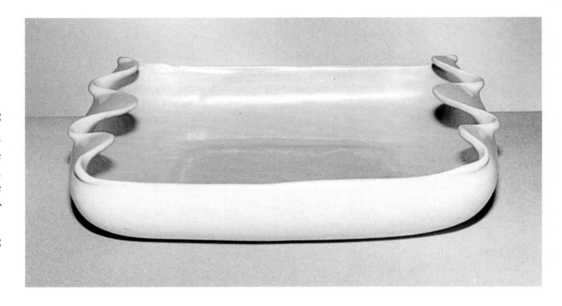

BOWL. #1409 - 8½", semi-matte white/green, ribbon-edge bowl, $22.00 – 28.00.

BOWL. #M1492 - 9½", semi-matte white, round footed bowl, $22.00 – 28.00. This bowl was ideal for floating flowers.

Compotes

COMPOTE. **#M1597 - 7"**, semi-matte white compote with medium pedestal, $24.00 – 28.00.

COMPOTE. **#690 - 9"**, semi-matte white fluted compote, $30.00 – 38.00. This compote was also produced in the 1960s in Red Wing's Steroline. It was a very attractive piece.

Planters

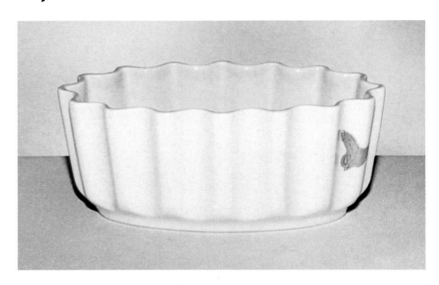

PLANTER. #770 - 7½", semi-matte white/green, silver wing label, ribbed planter, $28.00 – 36.00. The planters of the 1940s vintage, done in the semi-matte white, were quite elegant.

PLANTER. #1195 - 5", semi-matte white/green, round flower-handled planter, $30.00 – 38.00. This was the planter, that belonged to my mother, which led me to begin collecting Red Wing.

PLANTER. #896 - 7", semi-matte yellow/turquoise, tulip-shaped planter, $35.00 – 40.00. This planter also came in a 4" size. The color is different than most of the 1940s items. This piece almost has the look of a RumRill item.

Candleholders

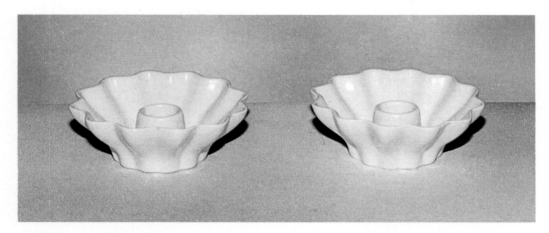

CANDLEHOLDERS. #1619 - 4½", semi-matte white, scallop edge candleholders, $18.00 – 26.00 pair. Most of the candleholders of this vintage were quite fancy and sold for quite a lot of money for the times. Ranging from $12.00 to $42.00 per pair. These two sets, however, were some of the plainer, less expensive candleholders.

CANDLEHOLDERS. #B1409 - 5", semi-matte white/ green, tear drop candleholders, $18.00 – 24.00 pair.

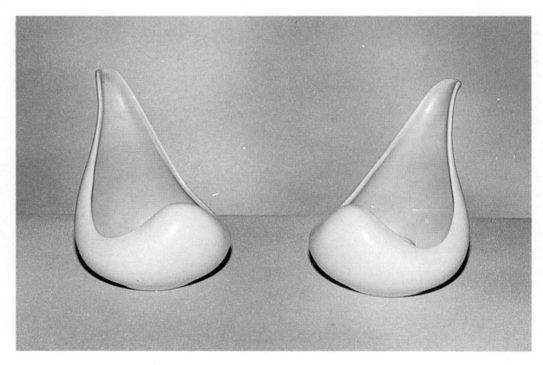

Console Sets

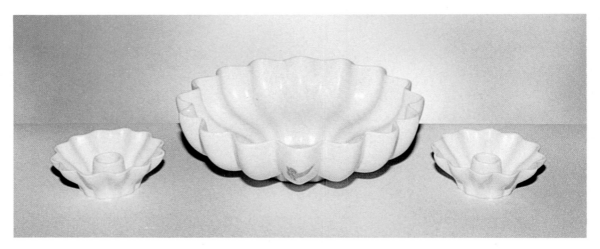

Console Set. #1620 - 10" bowl, #1619 - 4½" candleholders, semi-matte white, scallop-edge console set, $48.00 – 55.00.

Console Set. #1409 - 8½" bowl, #B1409 - 5" candleholders, swan figurine, semi-matte white/green, $46.00 – 52.00. Price is with swan insert.

Novelty Pieces

The art pottery of the 1940s had a variety of novelty pieces. There were assorted animal planters and small miniature vases and bowls. The novelty pieces are not seen very often.

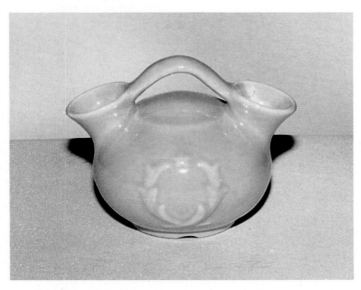

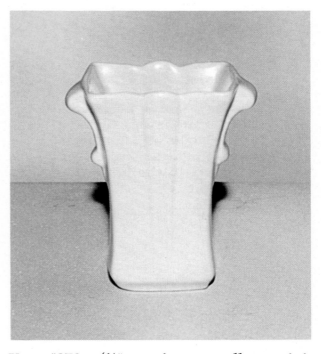

VASE. #908 - 4½, gloss pink, double hole mini-vase, $20.00 – 28.00. Notice that this piece in done in a gloss glaze. Probably made in the late 1940s when they were getting ready to start the gloss glazes that were used in the 1950s and 1960s.

VASE. #873 - 4½", semi-matte yellow, mini-vase, $20.00 – 24.00. It is hard to imagine what they put in these tiny vases. It is thought that many of these novelty items were made for use in a child's room.

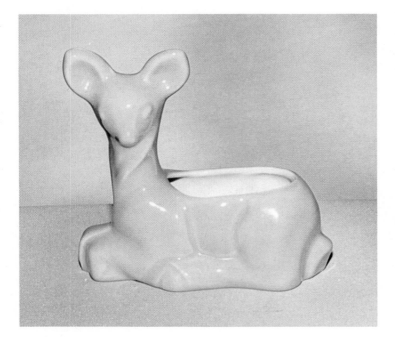

PLANTER. #1338 - 5½", gloss turquoise, deer planter, $32.00 – 38.00. Other animal planters included a horse, seal, teddy bear, duck, pig, rabbit, and fish. There were also some fruit shaped planters.

FIGURINE. #None - 6¾", semi-matte white, swan figurine insert, $8.00 – 12.00. These types of figurines were used as inserts in the bowls for decoration.

Color Chart

1940s

Art Pottery	Blue
	Matte White
	Pink
	Yellow
	Green
	Matte White - Green Lined
	Pink - White Lined
	Blue - White Lined
	Ivory - Brown Wipe
	Ivory - Green Wipe
	Green - White Lined

Note: Although is does not include all the colors of this vintage, it gives a good overview of them.

Art Pottery – 1950s & 1960s

In the 1950s and 1960s, Red Wing introduced a wide array of colors, along with a contemporary look in a lot of the pieces. They strayed from the traditional colors and shapes they used in the 1930s and 1940s.

As in previous years, some of the 1940s pottery was carried on into the early 1950s. But in the mid 1950s Red Wing introduced a variety of new art pottery. All done in a gloss glaze, most with the art deco look and style. The colors ranged from the traditional white to purple, produced in a lot of odd shaped pieces. Some of the art pottery of this period are not as easily recognized by sight, as was the earlier art ware.

Like any Baby Boomer knows, the 1950s and 1960s were a special time of many changes, and Red Wing was changing with them. The Red Wing art pottery had the look and aura of the times.

1950s Art Pottery

Continuing the trend started in the 1940s, the 1950s art pottery did not have a lot of line names. They were grouped in the Red Wing catalog by items, such as vases, bowls, compotes, and planters. The candleholders were usually put on the page with the matching console bowl. Red Wing did not make a lot of different candleholders. Most of them matched a bowl and were sold to form a console set. They also introduced many varieties of ashtrays, a cake salver, and large contemporary cornucopias. Along with these items they continued with the novelty planters, but introduced some unique pieces which will be shown later in this chapter.

The colors in the art pottery line were broadened to include a lot of bright glossy finishes on the pieces, such as pea green and burnt orange. They continued with the two-tone coloring, usually having a plain color on the inside that blended with the outside. Introduced in the mid 1950s were a line of fleck colors. The color was flecked with light black and was used for solid and with two-tone. There were several of these fleck colors, fleck yellow, fleck green, fleck zephyr pink, fleck Nile blue, and fleck orchid. The art ware done in these colors were quite attractive and modern looking. You do not find a lot of art pottery in these colors, and they tend to command higher prices, especially the fleck zephyr pink.

The pieces of art pottery on the following pages are 1950s vintage. Notice how the look of the pottery changed.

Vases

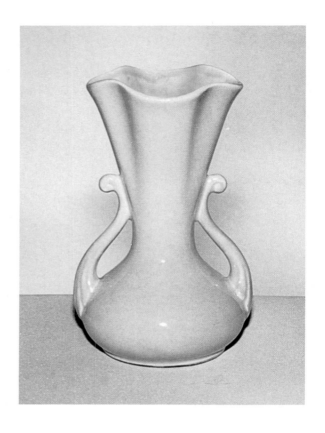

VASE. **#505 - 7½", gloss blue/pink, cloverleaf vase, $28.00 – 34.00. This vase and number was also produced in the 1930s and continued in a variety of colors on through the 1960s.**

VASE. **#M1442 - 8½", gloss fleck yellow snifter vase, $32.00 – 38.00. This is one the new fleck colors introduced and is hard to find. This vase was also produced in the 1940s in semi-matte white.**

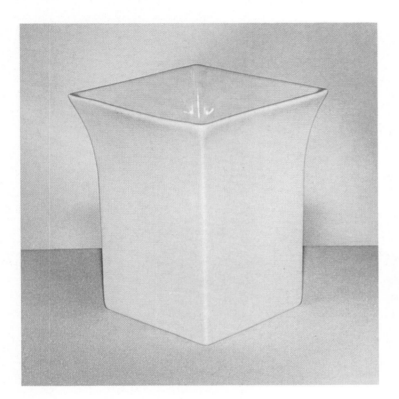

VASE. **#1553** - 6½", semi-matte white/green, Mandarin-type vase, $26.00 – 32.00.

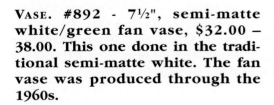

VASE. **#892** - 7½", semi-matte white/green fan vase, $32.00 – 38.00. This one done in the traditional semi-matte white. The fan vase was produced through the 1960s.

VASE. #1356 - 7½", gloss pea green/brown, snail-shaped vase, $26.00 – 34.00.

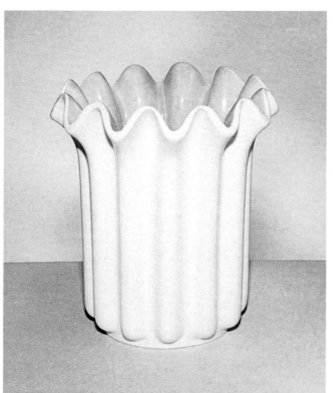

VASE. #1169 - 7½", semi-matte white/green, ribbon vase, $32.00 – 38.00. Sold from the 1940s through the 1960s, the green is a different shade than the 1940s vase.

VASE. #1097 - 5¾", gloss blue/yellow, silver wing label, cornucopia vase, $26.00 – 34.00. Sold in a semi-matte white in the 1940s.

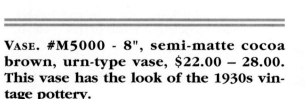

VASE. #M5000 - 8", semi-matte cocoa brown, urn-type vase, $22.00 – 28.00. This vase has the look of the 1930s vintage pottery.

VASE. #1162 - 9", gloss pea green/gray, vine-handled vase, $32.00 – 40.00. This vase was also part of a decorator line in the late 1930s, done in white with green vine decorations.

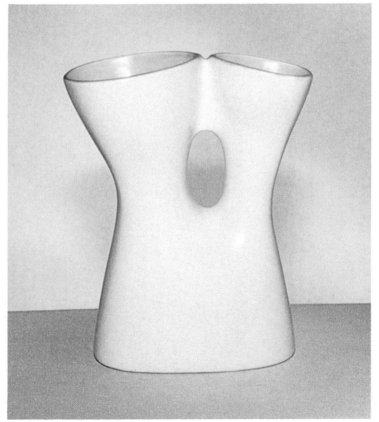

VASE. #B1427 - 8", semi-matte white/green, gladiolus vase, $26.00 – 32.00. This is one of the new type vases introduced in the 1950s. It was designed for gladiola flowers.

VASE. #B1425 - 8", gloss burnt orange/green, contemporary vase, $26.00 – 32.00.

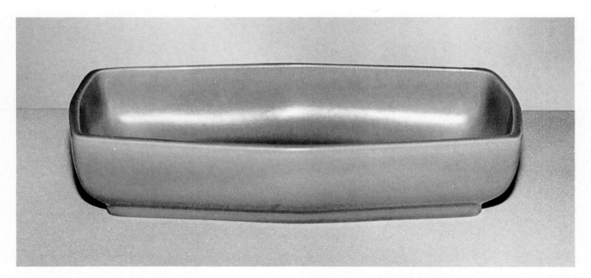

BOWL. #5019 - 9", semi-matte green, rectangle bowl, $24.00 – 28.00. Elegant looking in the green semi-matte color. It almost seems to have a touch of gloss in the glaze.

Compotes

COMPOTE. #5011 - 4½" x 6¾", semi-matte green, pedestal compote, $24.00 – 30.00. Like the bowl that matches, this is a very elegant looking compote.

Candleholders

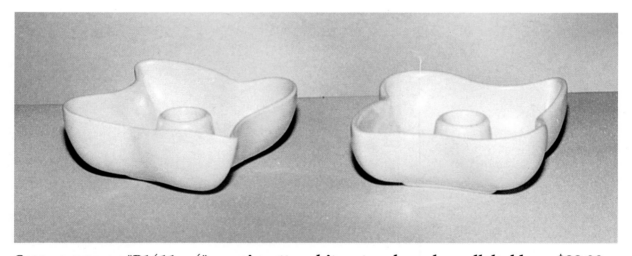

CANDLEHOLDERS. #B1411 - 4", semi-matte white, star-shaped candleholders, $22.00 – 28.00 pair. These candleholders were also part of a console set with a bowl of the same shape.

Decorator Brass Line

Introduced in 1958, this was one of the few lines of the 1950s vintage, and was the only line of Red Wing art pottery to be decorated with brass. There were several styles of pieces, different vases, different planters, and a compote. Done in a variety of colors including black and the fleck colors, this was very attractive art ware. Not seen often, these pieces of pottery tend to be expensive.

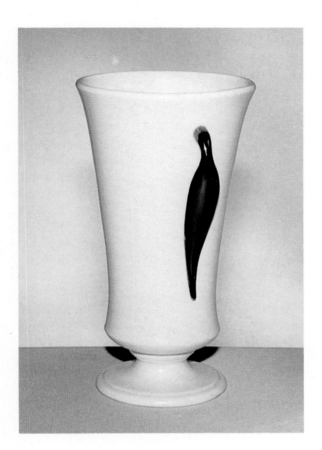

VASE. #M1609 - 10", semi-matte white, brass-handled vase, $40.00 – 50.00. The handles on both shaped vases were leaf designed. The brass was attached with screws through a hole placed in the pottery.

PLANTER. #M1612 - 10½ x 4¾", gloss fleck yellow, brass-trimmed planter, $45.00 – 56.00. The other planter was smaller and trimmed with loop-shaped brass instead of this leaf shape.

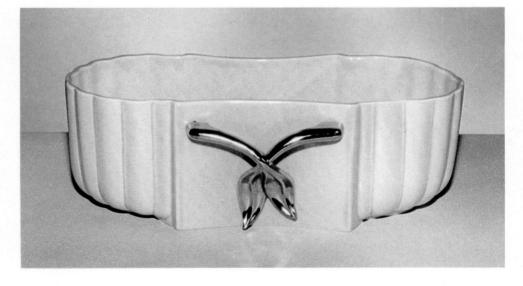

Decorator Glazed Line

Another decorator line of the 1950s was done in crystalline and crackle glazes. These glazes were accomplished by firing the pottery in different layers, firing once then covering the crackle or crystalline and firing again. It was quite a complicated process, but produced a totally different look to the pottery.

These pieces were known to come in ashtrays and vases, in blue, silver-green, and burnt orange. Not often found, these pieces also tend to be quite expensive.

VASE. 1301 - 5", gloss blue/gun metal, crackle vase, $45.00 – 60.00. The glaze on this vase was done in three stages and as you can see produced a very unique look.

Planters

The following pieces of art ware were some of the many varieties of planters produced in the 1950s. People must have used a lot of small planters in their homes considering the many different kinds that were made including novelty planters. They came in all different shapes, designs, and colors. When looking for Red Wing planters, you almost have to look at the bottom of any planter to determine if it is Red Wing. You can not tell most of them by appearance.

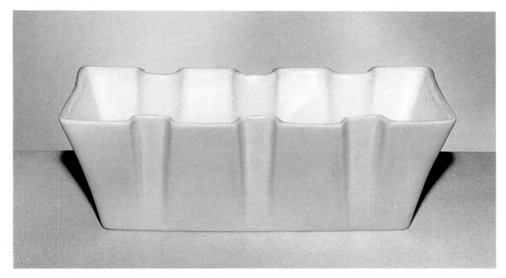

PLANTER. #1265 - 10", semi-matte green/white, greek-style planter, $22.00 – 26.00. By this period, there were very few pieces of art ware produced in the semi-matte glaze. However, Red Wing did continue to use this glaze on a few items through the 1960s.

PLANTER. #M1549 - 7", semi-matte white/green, rectangle footed planter, $20.00 – 26.00.

PLANTER. #1572 - 7", gloss maroon/light gray, rectangle planter, $24.00 – 30.00. This maroon color seems to be higher in price than some of the other colors of this vintage. There are also candleholders known to have been produced in the color.

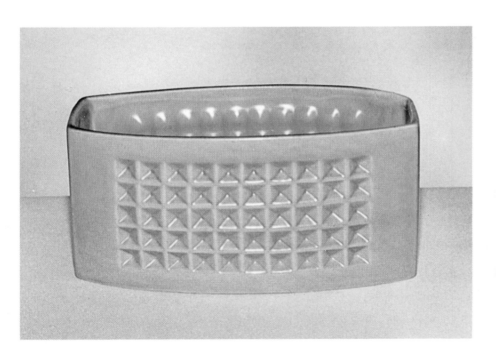

PLANTER. #1616 - 7½", semi-matte green, grid-embossed planter, $20.00 – 26.00.

Novelty Planters

Introduced in the late 1950s was a very unique line of novelty planters. They included a baby grand piano, a violin, a banjo, and a cart. These planters were done in great detail to look identical to the real thing. The planters were done in a variety of solid and flecked colors.

PLANTER. #M1484 - 13", gloss zephyr pink fleck, violin planter, $45.00 – 55.00. Notice they added rubber band strings to look realistic. The banjo also had rubber band strings.

PLANTER. #1484 - 13", semi-matte black, violin planter, $48.00 – 58.00. Art ware done in black is harder to find and commands higher prices. Again notice the rubber band strings.

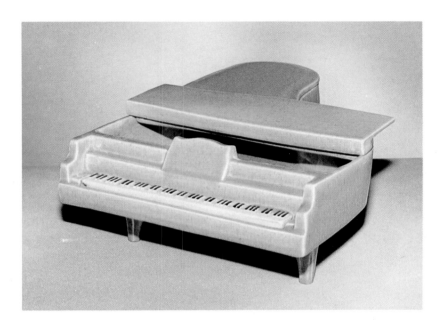

PLANTER. #M1525 - 10 x 9", gloss fleck yellow, baby grand piano planter, $240.00 – 350.00. The piano planters are one of the most sought-after items in the art pottery. In good condition, they command very high prices. The piano was also produced in black, which sells for considerably more than the other colors. Notice the detail on these pianos. As you can see, they even put little black and white keys on them. The top of the piano is removable.

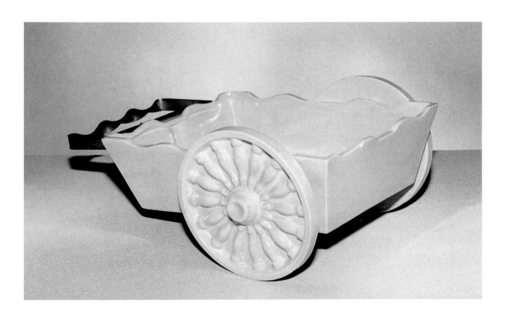

PLANTER. #M1531 - 9 x 7", semi-matte celadon yellow, cart planter, $45.00 – 70.00. As with the other planters, the cart was done in detail. Notice the brass handle. The wheels also go around.

Art Pottery 1960s

In the early 1960s, Red Wing continued grouping their art pottery in the catalog by item. Most of them were simply called miscellaneous, as in the 1950s. Some of the pieces from the past were carried on, like they had always done.

Then Red Wing went back to the style of giving line names to their art pottery. This practice gave the art ware a certain distinction as it did with the older lines. However, there were not as many line names given compared to the 1930s.

Red Wing categorized most of the art ware in lines. Some of the lines were Floraline, Stereoline, and Chromoline. They also introduced a Decorator Line and a Deluxe Line. The Decorator and Deluxe lines were quite ornate like some of their 1930s counterparts. One grouping was decorated with cherubs, the Deluxe pieces were highly decorated with ivy and swans. There was also a Prismatique Line, a Belle Line, and a Bronze Line. Red Wing also continued to produce the novelty planters and some other new and interesting items. Some of these will be shown later in the chapter. Like in the past they also had groups they simply called miscellaneous.

The colors of the 1960s continued to be bright and modern, but Red Wing gave them more specific names, such as cypress green, sagebrush, hyacinth, and butterscotch, to name a few. They also added orchid, coral, and many others. They did, however, continue the basic colors such as, matte white, black, and cocoa brown. Quite a lot of the pottery continued to be produced in the two-tone style.

The Red Wing catalogs of the 1950s and 1960s were done in spring and fall editions. The pottery number, description, size, and price of each were all listed on the page with pictures of the art ware. Colors were added or dropped from spring to fall. Not all colors were always available in a certain piece of pottery, but in the next edition there was a different color for the same piece of art ware. Each piece, at some time, was produced in many different colors.

Like in the 1950s, the art ware continued to have the bright contemporary look of the times, along with some of the plainer more distinguished looking pottery.

During the 1960s Red Wing continued producing their line of novelty planters, adding the new unusual pieces created in the late 1950s, such as the piano, banjo, and violin. They also continued with the line of children's planters which included a dachshund, donkey, owl, and giraffe.

The giraffe was 11" tall, brown with tan fleck, #896, designed by Charles Murphy. It was one of his favorite pieces. This giraffe planter was the commemorative piece for the 1995 Red Wing Collectors Society. Done in a 6" miniature with opposite colors, it was sold exclusively to members of the society at their yearly convention in Red Wing, MN.

Once you learn to recognize the look of the 1950s, you will also know the theme of the 1960s vintage. But you will always need to look at the bottom markings to identify the piece as Red Wing.

The pieces of art pottery on the following pages are 1960s vintage. Notice the continued look of the 1950s.

Floraline

The Red Wing Floraline consisted of vases, bowls, compotes, candleholders, and planters done in various colors, including cypress green, matte white, cinnamon, black, coral, and orchid. Most have a gloss finish. As you will notice by the letters preceding the numbers of the pottery, Belle Kogan and Charles Murphy designed a lot of the Floraline pieces.

VASE. #505 - 7½", semi-matte white/green, cloverleaf vase, $24.00 – 32.00. This vase was produced since the 1930s and placed in the Floraline of the 1960s.

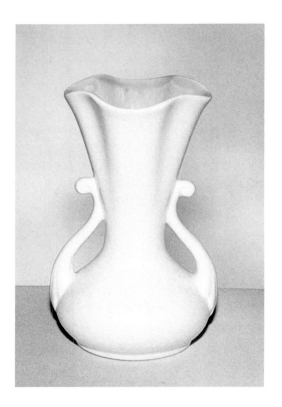

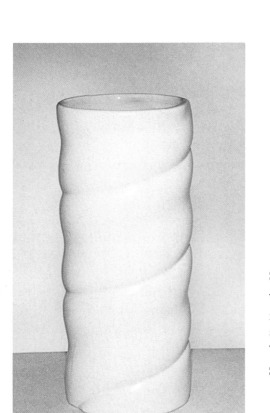

VASE. #1235 - 9¾", semi-matte white/green, spiral vase, $24.00 – 30.00. This was quite an attractive piece of pottery, the white color would have fit into any decor.

VASE. #1559 - 9½", gloss zephyr pink fleck, pitcher vase, $32.00 – 40.00. The zephyr pink fleck pieces command some of the higher prices of the 1950s and 1960s art pottery, possibly because of popularity or perhaps scarcity.

VASE. #416 - 10", semi-matte coral/ colonial buff, gladiolus vase, $58.00 – 72.00. This vase was designed to hold an arrangement of gladiola flowers. It also commands some of the higher prices of this vintage. As you can see it would be lovely with a colorful array of gladiolus fanned across. The vase also came in a #416 - 12" size and a variety of colors, including pink zephyr fleck.

VASE. #892 - 7½", gloss zephyr pink fleck, silver wing label, fan vase, $44.00 – 52.00. The flower arrangements in the fan vases would have looked similar to the gladiola vase.

VASE. #892 - 7½", gloss cypress green/coral, red wing label, fan vase, $38.00 – 46.00. Notice the different style of wing label on this vase.

VASE. #1512 - 7", semi-matte cypress green/yellow, long handled bud vase, $20.00 – 26.00.

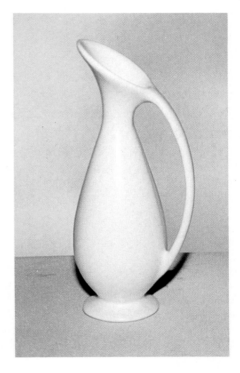

VASE. #1510 - 7", semi-matte white, long handled bud vase, $20.00 – 26.00.

VASE. #510 - 7½", semi-matte green, silver wing label, slender bud vase, $22.00 – 28.00. Notice how the wing label has lost most of its color from use.

VASE. #1621 - 8", gloss cocoa brown/yellow, silver wing label, square bud vase, $22.00 – 26.00.

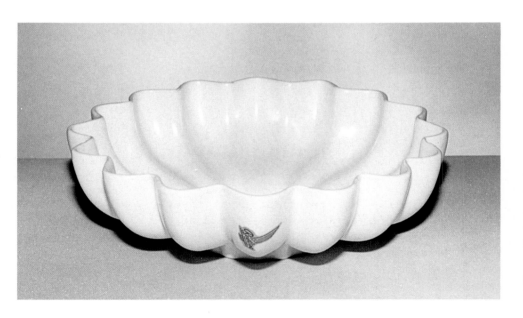

BOWL. #1620 - 10", semi-matte white, silver wing label, scallop-edge bowl, $35.00 – 44.00. The wing label on this bowl is in almost perfect condition, indicating that the bowl did not have much use. This bowl is also part of a console set with matching candleholders.

BOWL. #M1572 - 10 x 7", gloss fleck zephyr pink, novelty bowl with handle, $24.00 – 30.00.

BOWL. #M1447 - 12 x 5", semi-matte white, contoured bowl, $22.00 – 28.00. The contour design of this bowl is similar to a group of Red Wing called garden club bowls.

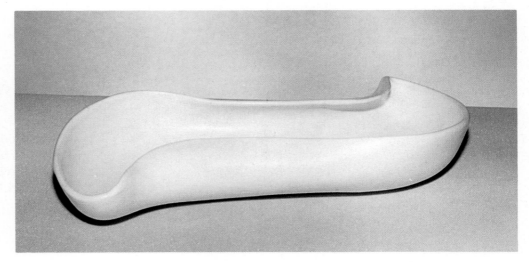

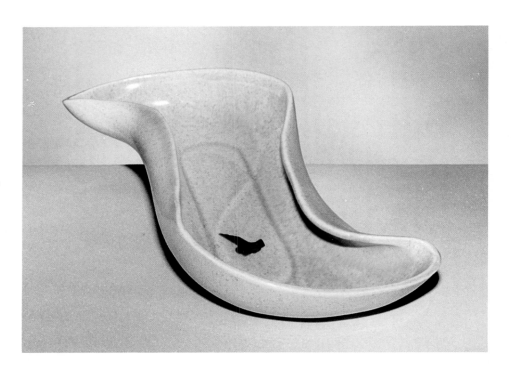

BOWL. #M1447 - 12 x 5", gloss fleck zephyr pink, gold wing label, contoured bowl, $24.00 – 32.00. Notice the placement of the wing label on the inside of the bowl, this was unusual. This bowl is identical except for color to the previous bowl.

BOWL. M5010 - 8", gloss fleck orchid, round footed bowl, $22.00 – 28.00. This is a very unusual color, it is hard to imagine in what setting this bowl would have been used. Not much of this fleck color is found.

BOWL. #M1492 - 10", gloss fleck green, round low footed bowl, $22.00 – 28.00. Again an odd and not-often-seen color.

COMPOTE. M1597 - 7", semi-matte white, medium pedestal compote, $22.00 – 28.00.

COMPOTE. #M5006 - 11", semi-matte white, contemporary low oval compote, $20.00 – 26.00.

COMPOTE. #635 - 11½ x 7", gloss cinnamon, cornucopia footed compote, $26.00 – 32.00. An interesting piece of pottery, this cornucopia has quite a bit of detail on the outside.

COMPOTE. **#M5005 - 10 x 6½", semimatte cocoa brown, tall oval compote, $22.00 – 26.00.**

PLANTER. **#B1403 - 5", gloss fleck zephyr pink, gold wing label, violet planter, $24.00 – 32.00. These violet planters originally came with a common red clay insert to plant the flowers in. This was not a common practice with the Red Wing planters.**

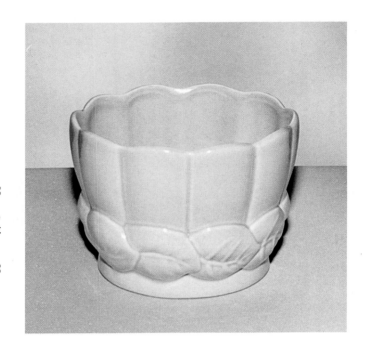

PLANTER. B1403 - 5", gloss gray, violet planter, $24.00 – 32.00. This planter is identical except for the color to the previous one.

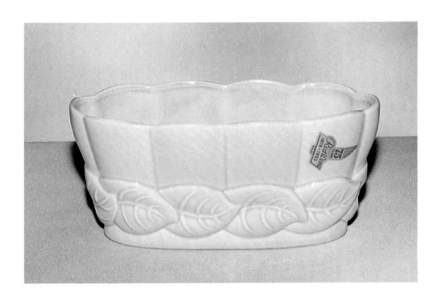

PLANTER. #1402 - 7½" x 3⅓", gloss lemon yellow/gray, gold wing label, rectangle planter, $30.00 – 38.00. Notice that the wing label is one of the 75th anniversary labels, dated 1878 – 1953.

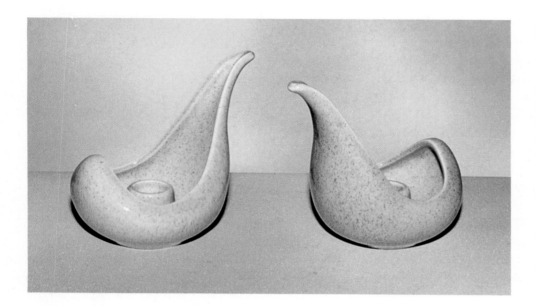

CANDLEHOLDERS. **#B1409 - 5", gloss fleck zephyr pink, tear drop candleholders, $20.00 – 28.00 pair. Although the same number and color, notice that on the right is a darker pink. These candleholders were not originally a pair. As mentioned earlier, the colors varied with each production run.**

CONSOLE SET. **M1572 - 10 x 7" bowl, #B1409 - 5" candleholders, fleck zephyr pink, console set, $45.00 – 58.00. The candleholders are not an original pair.**

Stereoline

The Red Wing Stereoline consisted of vases, bowls, compotes, candleholders, planters, ashtrays, and jardinieres. There were not a lot of vases in this line. The pottery in this line tended to be a little more ornate than the Floraline.

Colors of the pottery were the same as Floraline. However, Red Wing continued to add new colors in every shade you can imagine. By the mid 1960s there were many times more colors then in previous years. You can see a list of the colors at the end of this chapter. Most of the Steroline items were also available in the Decorator Line colors which were blue, silver green, and burnt orange.

VASE. #1440 - 6", semi-matte bronze green/pea green, tulip vase, $20.00 – 26.00. This was one of the unique colors introduced by Red Wing in the 1960s. The bronze color was placed over the green and refired. As you can see by the top of this vase, the edges were not always completely covered. This is one of the distinctive aspects of antique pottery. The pieces were not always perfect.

One of the other vases in the Steroline was decorated with the same leaf design, however the vase was 12" tall and a bulbous shape. There were also two styles of urn vases which were more ornate. They had loop handles with leaves on one end which rested on the vases. The outside of these vases was a ribbed style similar to the Belle Line which you will see on a following page.

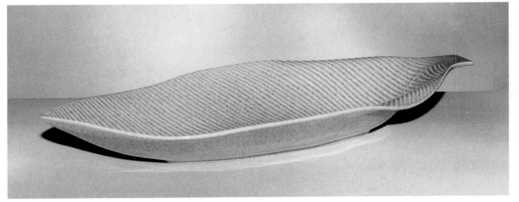

BOWL. #M1453 - 18", gloss fleck zephyr pink, long leaf bowl, $28.00 – 36.00. This bowl was part of a very modern looking console set along with candleholders to match.

BOWL. #670 - 5 x 6", semi-matte hyacinth, hat-shape bowl, $20.00 – 26.00. Another unique color done in the same manner as the bronze green. A purple overlay on a blue base created a very pretty glaze.

COMPOTE. #665 - 11", gloss burnt orange, wide boat compote, $26.00 – 32.00. This color indeed looks burnt. Notice the black spots in the glaze, they are especially large on the inside bottom of the bowl. The burnt orange was also used in the Decorator Line.

COMPOTE. #690 - 6 x 9", semi-matte white/green, ribbed fluted compote, $30.00 – 38.00. There was also a smaller #691 - 7½" compote identical to this one.

PLANTER. #1467 - 10½", gloss fleck Nile blue, silver wing label, hanging planter, $28.00 – 38.00. This planter originally came with a gold chain hooked in a hole at the top for hanging.

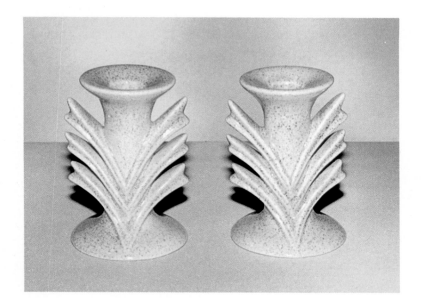

CANDLEHOLDERS. #M1471 - 4¾", gloss fleck zephyr pink, leaf-style candleholders, $24.00 – 30.00. These are also very modern looking pieces of pottery.

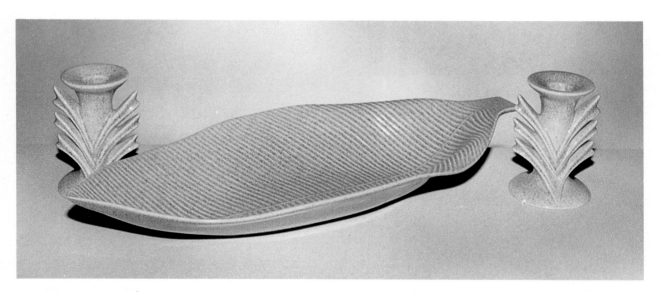

CONSOLE SET. #M1453 - 18" bowl, M1471 - 4¾" candleholders, gloss fleck zephyr pink, console set, $48.00 – 56.00. You can generally buy console sets for less money than the individual pieces. However, you do not often find them as a set. It can be fun to buy a piece from a set and then look for the matching piece or pieces.

Belle Line

The Belle Line was produced in a very limited number of pieces. These included vases, bowls, and compotes, each in one size. The vases ranged from 6" high to 12" high. They included an 8" fan vase and a 12" gladiolus vase. There was an oval bowl and compote and a tall compote. The line was ribbed at the bottom with a smooth collar at the top of each piece, giving them a contemporary look.

There were four colors, olive green/moss green, chocolate with white overlay, snow white/orange, and peacock blue/emerald green. Some of the pieces were done in a textured type glaze that was rough to the touch, others in a gloss glaze. Perhaps they were done at different times, or the line may have been available in both finishes. There does not seem to be much of the Belle Line around.

These pieces from the Belle Line show the style of the line, and the two different glazes used.

VASE. #842 - 8", matte snow white/orange, footed vase, $26.00 – 38.00. This vase is an example of the textured matte used on the Belle Line, with a traditional matte glaze on the inside.

COMPOTE. #848 -10", gloss peacock blue/emerald green, medium footed compote, $22.00 – 30.00. This piece has the gloss glaze that was also used in the Belle Line. Notice the unusual color combination designed to fit in the decor colors of the 1960s.

Prismatique Line

The Prismatique Line was very eye catching, all having distinguished geometrical prism shapes and glazed with bright colors. The line consisted of vases, bowls, compotes, and planters. Some were rounded and others had straight angles.

The colors were lemon yellow/white, Persian blue/white, white/orange, mandarin orange/white, celadon/mandarin orange. Some pieces were also done in a different combination of these colors.

The following pieces show the straight angle style of the Prismatique Line and the bright colors used.

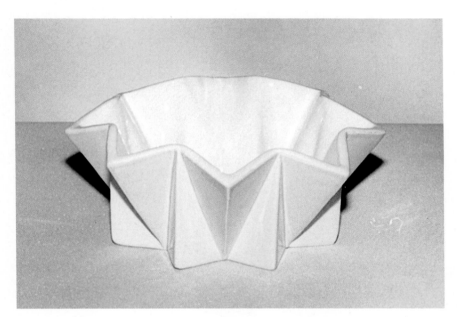

BOWL. #791 - 6", gloss Persian blue/white, shallow bowl, $26.00 – 32.00. Though hard to find, the Persian blue is one of the colors that seems to be more readily found.

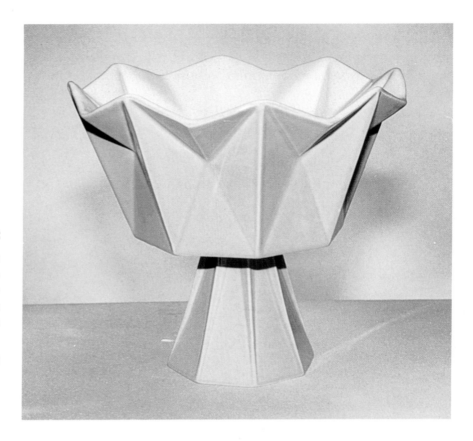

COMPOTE. #796 - 8 x 9½", gloss Persian blue/white, large compote, $42.00 – 58.00. Eye-catching in the Persian blue and almost 5" deep, this was a very large compote.

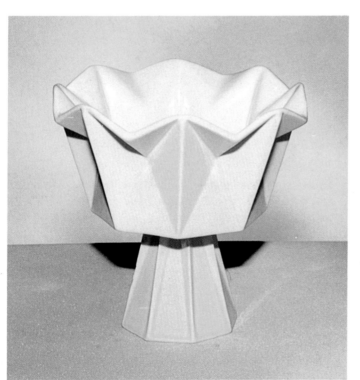

COMPOTE. #787 - 6 x 6½", gloss lemon yellow/white, straight angle compote $35.00 – 46.00. Identical except for size to the larger compote, this Prismatique piece was also very attractive.

Textura

Textura was produced in only three different pieces, a vase, bowl, and candleholder. The candleholders were sometimes called candlesticks in the Red Wing catalog. There was also a bird figurine to go in the bowls for added decoration. The bowl and candleholders also formed console sets.

The pottery came in a variety of color combinations, but in only one size and style of each item. The vase #B2112 was 8" tall, and had a contoured oblong shape. All the pieces had the same lined texture glaze on the outside.

This art ware appeared in the spring 1963 Red Wing catalog. It is hard to tell how long it was produced or if other pieces were added. Like a lot of the other 1960s pottery, it was quite unique.

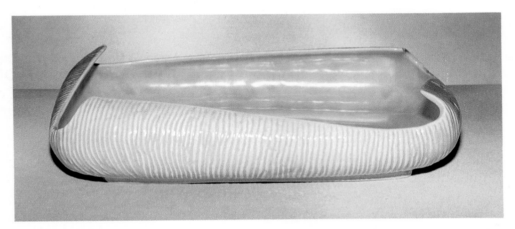

BOWL. B2110 - 14½", gloss gray/pink, console bowl, $28.00 – 38.00. The lines on this bowl are raised forming the texture glaze. It would seem the Textura was designed by Belle Kogan, since all the numbers are preceded by a B.

BOWL. #B2110 - 14½", gloss forest green/ lemon yellow, console bowl, $28.00 – 38.00. Identical to its gray counterpart except for color, the forest green and yellow was quite striking.

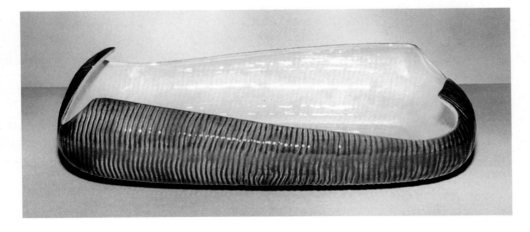

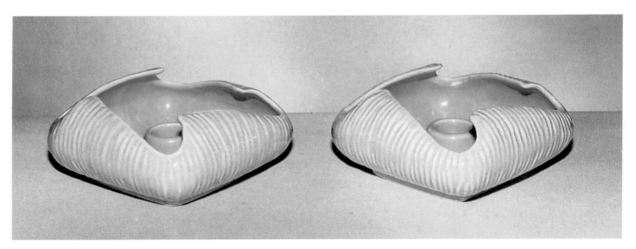

CANDLEHOLDERS. #B2111 - 5 x 5", gloss gray/pink, square candleholders, $20.00 – 26.00 pair. Called candlesticks, these were sold separately in the Red Wing catalog like most of the 1950s and 1960s candleholders.

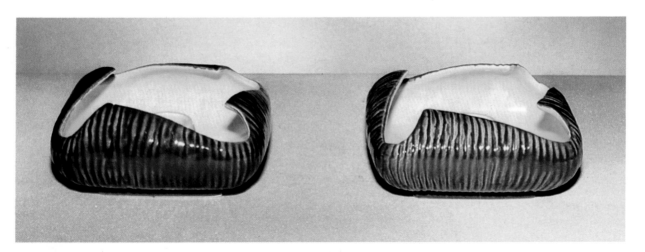

CANDLEHOLDERS. B2111 - 5 x 5", gloss forest green/lemon yellow, square candleholders, $20.00 – 26.00 pair. Identical to the gray set, they also were used as part of a console set.

FIGURINE. 10", gloss forest green, perched bird figurine, $15.00 – 22.00. Used as a centerpiece in the bowls, this bird has the same texture on the wings and tail as the outside of the bowl and candleholders.

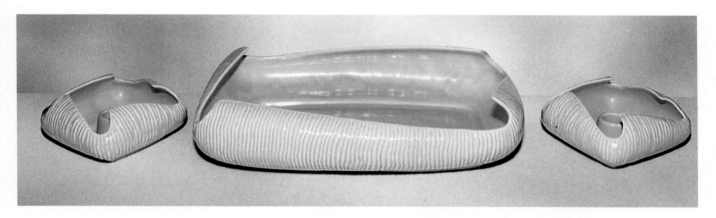

CONSOLE SET. #B2110 - 14½" bowl, B2111 5 x 5" candleholders, gloss gray/pink, Textura console set, $42.00 – 58.00. These console sets would have taken quite a large space to display.

CONSOLE SET. B2110 - 14½" bowl, B2111 5 x 5" candleholders, 10" bird figurine, gloss forest green/lemon yellow, Textura console set, $50.00 – 65.00 with bird figurine. Notice how the bird centerpiece gives the console set an added dimension. With flowers in the bowl and candles, it would be very attractive.

Tropicana

Named for their tropical look, the Tropicana Line came in a variety of vases, bowls, and planters. There was also a 13" window box bowl. The vases came in sizes ranging from 8" to 14". The planters were 8" and 10" long. All the pottery was decorated in one of three different embossed styles. There was Desert Flower, Shell Ginger, and Bird of Paradise.

The art ware came in various two-tone colors. The Tropicana art ware items are not plentiful, but some can be found. This line was known to have been sold in the 1963 and 1964 Red Wing catalogs.

VASE. #B2001 - 8", gloss gun metal gray/pea green, Shell Ginger, Tropicana vase, $32.00 – 44.00. This gun metal color is hard to find and commands a higher price than the other colors.

The design on the Bird of Paradise pieces had several leaves identical to the leaves on the Shell Ginger. Inside the leaves was a Bird of Paradise flower with the long center of the flower laying sideways. At a distance, it appears to be a scorpion-type bug on the art ware. This style of Tropicana definitely had a tropical look.

BOWL. #B2012 - 13", gloss forest green/lemon yellow, Desert Flower, Tropicana bowl, $24.00 – 30.00. This bowl had a similar style to the garden club bowls that are pictured later in the chapter.

PLANTER. #B2017 - 8", gloss forest green/lemon yellow, Shell Ginger, Tropicana planter, $22.00 – 28.00.

Chromoline

The Chromoline was one of the most attractive lines of art ware Red Wing made in the 1950s and 1960s. All the pieces had a smooth modern style and the color was hand painted on the pottery. The art ware was finished in a gloss glaze in only two colors.

The colors were a rust and green combination, and a blue and yellow combination. Hand painted on the pottery, they had the appearance of water colors, with a slight running which made the colors look blended together instead of straight lines.

Produced in the early 1960s this line included vases, bowls, and compotes. The line also contained 6" candleholders, ashtrays, and two sizes of candy dishes with lids. Hardly ever found, the Chromoline tends to command considerably higher prices than some of the other art ware.

VASE. #637 - 8", gloss blue/yellow combination, footed Chromoline vase, $42.00 – 56.00. This vase also came in a 10" size. Notice the rings of colors, all hand painted on the vase. The blue on the inside gets lighter on down in the vase, as if applied thinner than the top of the vase. The coloring on this vase is very appealing. As you can see, all the items in this line would have been very attractive.

Birch Bark Line

This was a very unique line made to resemble pieces of Birch wood. Produced in the early 1960s it was made in only four pieces. There was a canoe, two planters, and a vase. The vase was 7½" high, the canoe came in three sizes ranging from 10" to 17" long, and the planter came in a round 4" high size along with a log-shaped planter that was 11" long.

The finish on the art ware was a semi-matte glaze in a tan and brown wipe. It looked very similar to the earlier ivory and brown wipe items with a plain cinnamon brown color on the inside. Red Wing called it a Birch Bark finish and it was the only one available. Birch Bark pieces are not often seen and usually are higher priced than most.

The canoe was an unusual piece of pottery. Shaped identical to a real canoe, it is hard to say for what intended use they were produced, perhaps as a planter. The 17" long canoe sold for $5.00 in the fall of 1961. This was quite a lot of money for the times.

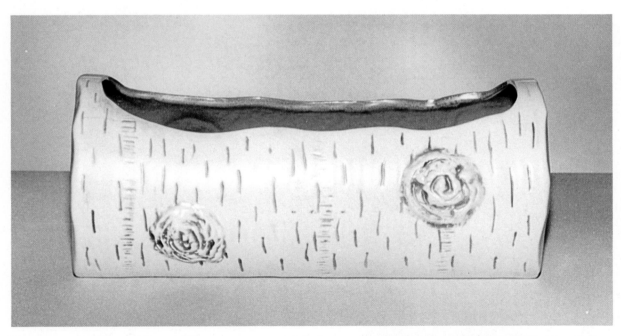

PLANTER. #730 - 11", semi-matte tan with brown wipe/cinnamon, Birch Bark log planter, $36.00 – 48.00. Notice the realistic detail they used in order to give this planter the look of a real log. All the pieces in this line had the same look as this planter.

Miscellaneous 1960s

As in previous years, Red Wing grouped many items simply under miscellaneous in their catalog. The groupings were simply labeled vases, console sets, bowls, and planters. The following pieces of art ware fell into that category in the 1960s Red Wing catalogs.

VASE. M1497 - 10", gloss fleck yellow/ice green, gold wing label, footed bulbous vase, $32.00 – 38.00. Notice the wing label is in perfect condition indicating the vase was not used or washed much. **Probably designed by Charles Murphy because of the M before the number.**

VASE. #1359 - 7¾", gloss cocoa brown/sagebrush, coffee cup handled vase, $26.00 – 35.00. Notice the unusual look of this vase, like coffee cups stacked one on top of another.

VASE. #401 - 7½", gloss lemon yellow/gray, cattail-embossed vase, $28.00 – 36.00. Notice the elegant detail on this vase, similar to the look of the 1930s except the gloss glaze.

VASE. #437 - 8", gloss fleck green/colonial buff, contoured vase, $22.00 – 28.00. This vase has a real contemporary look.

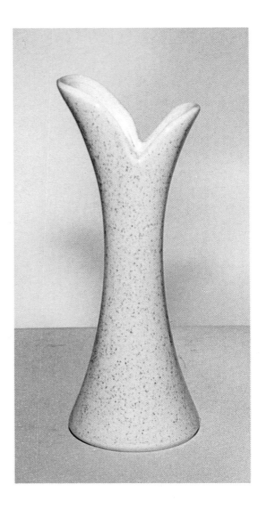

VASE. **#434 - 8¼", gloss fleck Nile blue/colonial buff, bud vase, $24.00 – 30.00. You will not find as many bud vases in the art ware.**

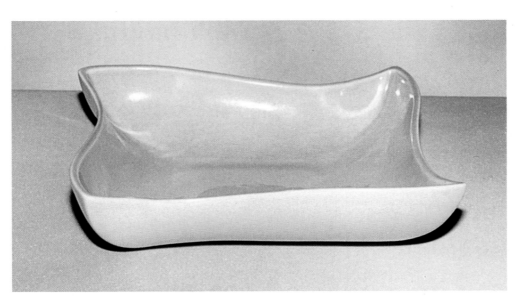

BOWL. **#1370 - 7", gloss lemon yellow/gray, star-shaped bowl, $24.00 – 30.00. This bowl probably also came in a larger size with candleholders to match.**

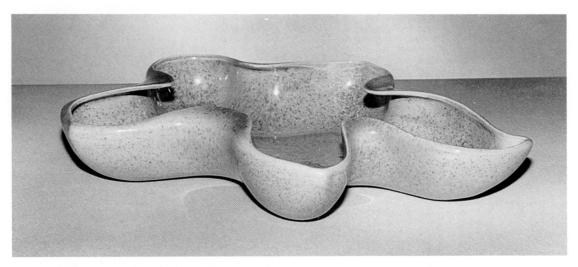

BOWL. #1407 - 12¾", gloss fleck Nile blue, leaf-shape bowl, $28.00 – 35.00. This bowl was part of a console set with tear drop candleholders, like the zephyr pink pair pictured earlier. The Nile blue is not a common color to find.

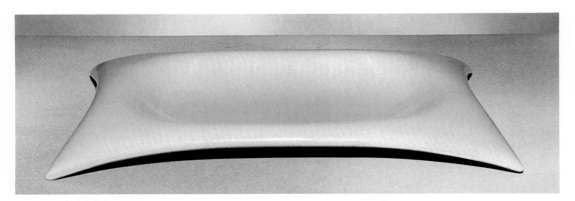

BOWL. #1333 - 13½ x 8", gloss forest green/lemon yellow, rectangle contemporary bowl, $24.00 – 30.00. This bowl was part of a console set with #1384 - 4½" square candleholders to match. It is hard to see the green color on these pieces because they are so low and the edges come out over the base.

101

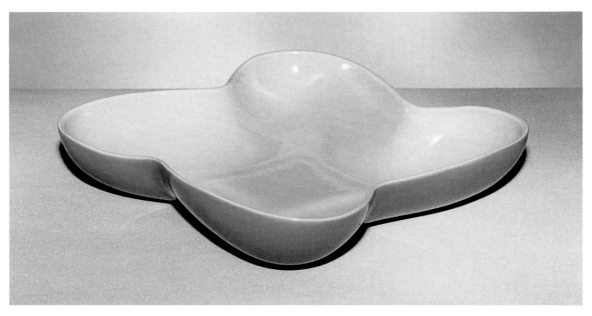

BOWL. #1412 - 8", gloss burnt orange/lime green, cloverleaf bowl, $24.00 – 32.00. This bowl was part of a console set with flat teardrop-shaped candleholders to match.

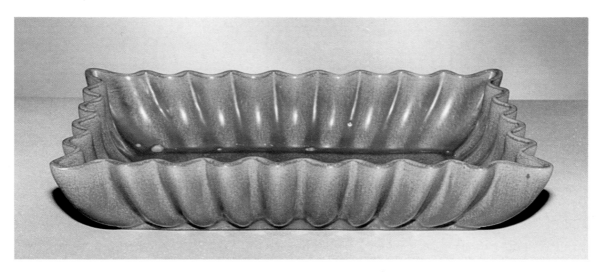

BOWL. #M1486 - 10¾", gloss cinnamon, ribbon bowl, $22.00 – 28.00. Notice the pits where the glaze had bubbled and later cracked off the bowl. Like all collectibles, not all pieces of this vintage were produced perfect.

BOWL. #B2015 - 12", gloss burnt orange/tan, shell-shaped garden club bowl, $24.00 – 32.00. The garden club bowls were designed by Belle Kogan for use by ladies belonging to a garden club. They had their own distinct style.

BOWL. #B2013 - 13", gloss pea green/forest green, gondola-style garden club bowl, $24.00 – 30.00. Another style only used in the garden club bowls.

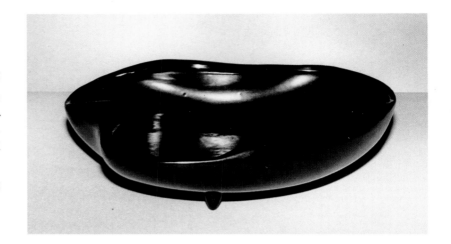

BOWL. #M1491 - 12", semi-matte black, contoured bowl, $28.00 – 36.00. Designed by Charles Murphy, the black color is hard to find and commands higher prices.

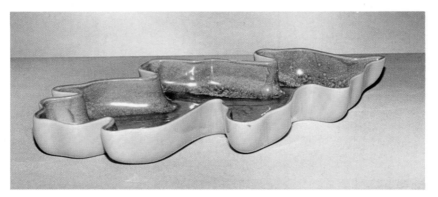

BOWL. 428 - 14 x 8", gloss pea green/caramel, leaf window box bowl, $26.00 – 32.00. Notice the color on the inside of the bowl, it was put on lightly so that the green showed through and actually gives the brownish green look of a leaf. These bowls were called window box bowls, and must have been used to place flowers in a window or window box. The next picture shows the detail on the bottom of these bowls.

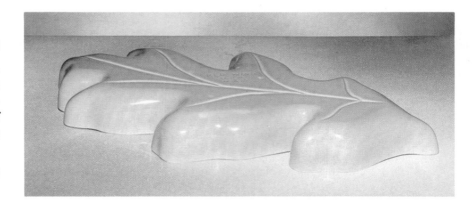

WINDOW BOX BOWL BOTTOM. Notice the detail they put on the leaf bowl. They have hand-drawn veins on the bottom of all these bowls. This was done before the glaze and firing.

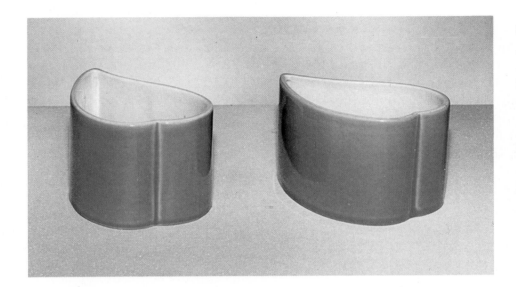

CANDLEHOLDERS. B1412-A - 4½", gloss burnt orange/ lime green, flat teardrop candleholders, $20.00 – 26.00 Pair. These candleholders came with a brass insert in the holes. Notice the number. It is quite unusual with an "A" following, indicating they are part of a console set

CONSOLE SET. #B1412 - 8" bowl, B1412-A - 4½" candleholders, gloss burnt orange/green console set, $35.00 – 45.00. The numbering on this console set is very unusual, it is rarely seen. The bowl and the candleholders have the same number with the letter A following the number on the candleholders. Most numbers on the console sets are different for the bowl and candleholders.

ASHTRAYS

Red Wing produced numerous styles and sizes of ashtrays in the 1950s and 1960s. They were glazed in a number of different colors, among them were the Decorator Line colors of blue, silver green, and burnt orange. Some of the other colors used were radiant orange, metallic brown, and caramel gold.

They also produced some unusual and unique ashtrays, such as fish and horse heads. There was also a specialty set called Grand Slam. This set consisted of four small ashtrays each shaped like a suit of playing cards. The spade and club were black. The heart and diamond were radiant orange. Rarely ever found, it would be a very good item to have in your collection.

The following are just a few of the many ashtrays made by Red Wing. There were a lot produced in much larger sizes, some they called man size.

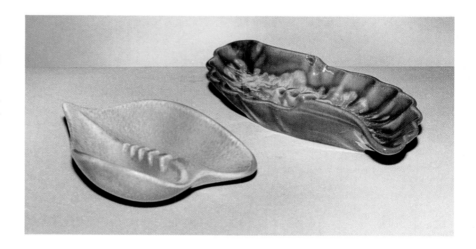

**ASHTRAYS. Right #828 - 9½",
gloss silver green, contoured
leaf-shape ashtray, $15.00 –
20.00. Left #741 - 6", gloss
caramel gold, contoured heart-
shape ashtray, $15.00 – 20.00.**

**ASHTRAY. #863 - 5½", gloss radiant
orange, book ashtray, $15.00 – 20.00.
This is one of the unusual style of ashtray made by Red Wing.**

SMALL PLANTERS

These small planters were also produced in the 1930s and 1940s. They are unusual because they have no bottom number. The only bottom marking is Red Wing. However small, they were quite dainty and attractive planters.

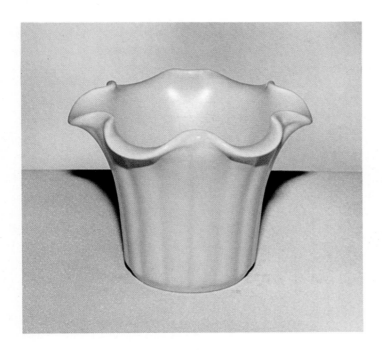

PLANTER. #None - 4", semi-matte turquoise, violet planter, $20.00 – 26.00. Notice the glaze on this piece is quite similar to the RumRill turquoise glaze. This color on the entire piece was not used much on Red Wing items.

PLANTER. #None - 4", semi-matte white/turquoise, violet planter, $20.00 – 26.00.

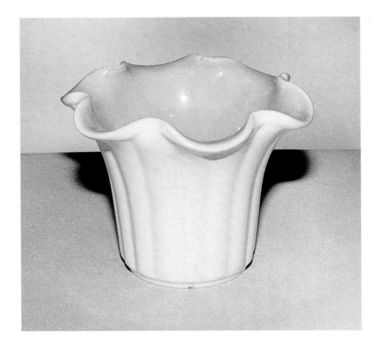

Color Chart
1950s & 1960s

Art Pottery:
- Matte White
- Gray
- Cypress Green
- Cinnamon
- Black
- Sagebrush
- Hyacinth
- Orchid
- Coral
- Blue
- Butterscotch
- Bronze Green
- Ice Green
- Walnut Green
- Cocoa Brown
- Lemon Yellow - Gray Lined
- Matte White - Green Lined
- Coral - Colonial Buff Lined
- Walnut Green - Coral Lined
- Forest Green - Yellow Lined
- Light Gray - Pink Lined
- Gun Metal - Pea Green Lined
- Cypress Green - Yellow Lined
- Cocoa Brown - Yellow Lined

Fleck Colors:
- Fleck Zephyr Pink
- Fleck Nile Blue
- Fleck Yellow
- Fleck Green
- Fleck Nile Blue - Colonial Buff Lined

Decorator Line:
- Crystalline Glaze
- Blue
- Silver Blue
- Burnt Orange

Prismatique Line:
- Lemon Yellow - White Lined
- Persian Blue - White Lined
- Celadon - Mandarin Orange Lined
- Mandarin Orange - White Lined
- White - Mandarin Orange Lined

Belle Line:
- Olive Green - Moss Green Lined
- Chocolate With White Overlay
- Snow White - Orange Lined
- Peacock Blue - Emerald Green Lined

Chromoline:
- Rust Combination
- Blue Combination

Ashtrays:
- Silver Green
- Radiant Orange
- Metallic Brown
- Caramel Gold

Note: Although this does not include all the colors of this vintage, it gives a good overview of them.

A Glance at Stoneware

Red Wing Stoneware dates back to 1861, when a German immigrant J. Pohl, a potter by trade, settled in north Goodhue Township. He shaped toys, bowls, jugs, crocks, and other items from clay he found on his farm and sold them to the local people. Pohl left after the Civil War, but is credited with having discovered that the clay in that region could be used to make stoneware.

In 1878 a group of Red Wing's early industrialists, knowing the rich clay from the pits near Goodhue was good enough to use to make stoneware, built the Red Wing Stoneware Company.

The early stoneware came in a variety of items, such as crocks, bowls, jars, and churns. There were many other items also produced. Housekeepers of the day bought their molasses and vinegar in the jugs, made butter in the churns, and used the five, 10, and 20 gallon crocks to make pickles, sauerkraut, and salt pork. In the commercial world, jugs and jars were used extensively for chemical containers.

After seeing Red Wing's success, several competitors emerged. Two of these were Northstar Stoneware Company and Minnesota Stoneware Company. Eventually the three companies merged, with Red Wing and Minnesota later bought out Northstar. Therefore, you will find stoneware with several bottom markings including, Red Wing Stoneware CO, Minnesota Stoneware CO, Northstar, and Red Wing Union Stoneware Company. Union Stoneware was an outlet for the other potters.

At one time Red Wing Stoneware Company was the largest producer of stoneware in the country. But with the introduction of the art pottery in 1936 and the depletion of the clay used to make stoneware as the country emerged from World War II, the stoneware line was discontinued. Red Wing Potteries, the name adopted in 1936 for the production on the art pottery, continued to make art ware until 1967.

There is very little stoneware that is not marked, with the exception of the early salt glazed stoneware, which have the well-known dark blue butterfly, Ps, birch leaves, or other markings on the face of the stoneware. Most stoneware is marked on the bottom or on the face of the item with the company name. Red Wing's crocks and jugs are known for the size number, a red wing, and circle stamp, all on the face of the pottery.

The stoneware produced at Red Wing Stoneware Company is favored by most collectors of stoneware. It continues to hold a very special place in the history of the era.

The following pages are a brief look at some of the stoneware produced by Red Wing.

Shoulder Jugs

The white shoulder jugs produced by Red Wing came in 3, 4, and 5 gallon sizes. Most jugs you will find are marked on the face with a red wing and a number which indicated the size of the jug. The wing was added to jugs and crocks in 1909. They also had a circle stamp with the name in the middle, usually "Red Wing Union Stoneware Co., Red Wing Minn." The size of the wings vary due to the fact that during World War II the size was reduced considerably because of the cost of the red dye used to make them. These jugs were used to store liquor and other liquids in large quantities.

WING SHOULDER JUG. **5-gallon, face marked, #5 large red wing, circle stamped, "Red Wing Union Stoneware Co. Red Wing Minn," $70.00 – 90.00. These jugs were not usually bottom marked, but some have been found with both face and bottom markings. Notice the cork in the jug. All of the shoulder jugs originally came with a cork in them. The corks were either lost or pushed down inside the jug.**

WING SHOULDER JUG. **5-gallon, face marked #5 large red wing, circle stamped, "Red Wing Union Stoneware Co, Red Wing Minn," $70.00 – 90.00. The large red wing dates this jug from 1909 to prior to World War II in the 1940s. Small wings were used during the war period. Notice the different shapes of these jugs, although both are five gallon, one is taller and thinner.**

WING SHOULDER JUG. 4-gallon, face marked, #4 large red wing, circle stamped, "Red Wing Union Stoneware Co., Red Wing Minn," $80.00 – 100.00. The four gallon jugs are harder to find and therefore command higher prices than the five- and three-gallon sizes.

WING SHOULDER JUG. 3-gallon, face marked, #3 large red wing, circle stamped, "Red Wing Union Stoneware Co., Red Wing Minn," $70.00 – 85.00. As a set these jugs make an attractive setting.

Crocks

The wing crocks produced by Red Wing were marked identically to the shoulder jugs, some having the large wings, some small wings. The wings were made smaller during the period of World War II for the same reasons as the jugs.

These crocks came in sizes from 2 gallons to 60 gallons. However, there were not very many of the large sizes produced. The early crocks can be identified by the large red wing and the fact they have no handles. Beginning in 1915 the crocks from 4 through 30 gallons were available with bail handles.

Putting the red wing on the crocks and jugs was considered a masterpiece of all times. It gave the Red Wing products unmistakable identification. No other stoneware manufacturer ever decorated with any colors except blue or black.

The following are examples of the smaller wing crocks. Notice the red wings and circle stamps.

WING CROCK. 3-gallon, face marked, #3 large red wing, circle stamped, "Red Wing Union Stoneware Co., Red Wing Minn," $50.00 – 60.00. Notice the large red wing and large circle stamp. This dates the crock to prior to World War II.

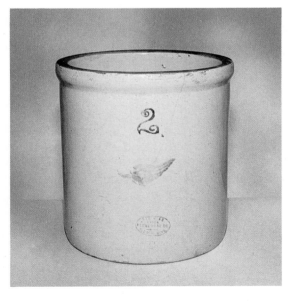

WING CROCK. 2-gallon, face marked, #2 small red wing, circle stamped, "Red Wing Union Stoneware Co., Red Wing Minn," $45.00 – 55.00. Notice the small red wing and small circle stamp, which dates the crock to the World War II period.

Small Jugs, Wax Sealers & Butter Jars

Red Wing Stoneware Co. and Minnesota Stoneware Company produced many of the same items. Their jugs, wax sealers, and butter jars were very similar except for the bottom markings. Each company bottom marked the stoneware with their name in several different versions.

The following are a few of the different stoneware pieces produced by both companies. You will notice very little difference between the two products.

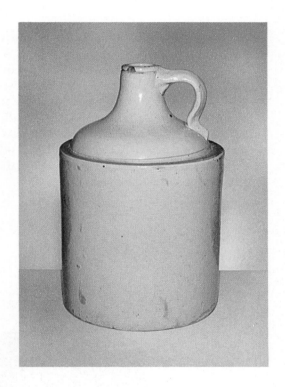

MINNESOTA STANDARD WHITE SHOULDER JUG. 1-gallon size, bottom marked, "Minnesota Stoneware Co., Red Wing Minn," $40.00 – 50.00. These jugs came in 1-quart, ½-gallon, and 1-gallon sizes. They were used to store liquids.

MINNESOTA BROWN COMMON JUG. ½-gallon size, bottom marked "Minnesota Stoneware Co., Red Wing Minn," $55.00 – 75.00. These jugs came in 1-quart, ½-gallon, and 1-gallon sizes.

113

MINNESOTA WAX SEALER. 1-quart, bottom marked "Minnesota Stoneware Co., Red Wing Minn," $60.00 – 65.00. The sealers came in 1-quart, ½-gallon, and 1-gallon sizes. They were used by the housekeepers of the period to can their vegetables, fruit, and other food items that needed to be sealed. The sealers originally came with stone or tin lids, which were placed on top of the sealer and wax was poured around the lid.

RED WING WAX SEALER. 1-quart, bottom marked "Red Wing Stoneware Co.," $40.00 – 55.00. The Red Wing sealers also came in 1-quart, ½-gallon, and 1-gallon size. Notice that except for the dark glaze around the rim, it is almost identical to the Minnesota sealer.

MINNESOTA WAX SEALER. ½-gallon, bottom marked "Minnesota Stoneware Co., Red Wing Minn.," $45.00 – 55.00. You will most often find the 1-quart sealers. However, you will occasionally see the ½-gallon size. The 1-gallon size seems to be scarce.

WAX SEALER LID. Marked #5, 3" stoneware button lid, $20.00 – 25.00. These are the lids that were used on the wax sealers. They were also used on snuff jars and were often interchangeable. Not all of the lids had a number on them.

MINNESOTA HIGH BUTTER JAR. ½-gallon, bottom marked "Minnesota Stoneware Co., Red Wing Minn.," $45.00 – 55.00. The butter jars also came in a low larger diameter size. Both shapes came in 1-quart, ½-gallon, and 1-gallon size.

RED WING HIGH BUTTER JAR. 1-quart, bottom marked "Red Wing Stoneware Co.," $40.00 – 50.00. You have probably noticed that the Minnesota Stoneware items command a higher price. This is because there were not nearly as many produced as Red Wing, so they are not as easily found.

Poultry Drinking Fountain

The poultry drinking fountains date back to the early salt glaze period. These fountains were used to give water or other liquids to poultry. They originally came with a base that was a larger diameter and allowed the liquid to seep out to the rim. When the poultry drank the liquid around the edge, more seeped out from the unit. These drinking fountains came in ½-gallon, 1-gallon, and 2-gallon sizes.

Red Wing advertised the drinking fountains by saying that they would save the farmer money because young chickens could not drown. They also sold the fact that the water was always clean because the chickens could not get in the small rim of the fountain.

**RED WING POULTRY DRINKING FOUNTAIN.
½-gallon, face stamped "Red Wing Poultry Drinking Fount And Buttermilk Feeder," without bottom plate, $45.00 – 55.00. These fountains are not usually found with the bottom plate. They are often missing due to outside use which led to breakage.**

Bowls

Red Wing produced several colors of paneled mixing bowls. They ranged in size from 6" to 11". A 5" size was later added and is a rare find. The colors were blue, brown, and a blue and reddish brown spongeware, so called because the colors were dabbed on the outside of the stoneware with a sponge. There were a few other colors of the spongeware, but this was the most popular. They are very attractive and a favorite among collectors. A complete set of these spongeware bowls is quite a valued collection.

Red Wing also produced a set of bowls they called Greek Key salad bowls, named after the Greek design used on the bowls. They came in sizes 6" through 12" in a blue and gray color and also brown. The Greek bowls are also quite a popular item among collectors.

Several other types of bowls were produced by Red Wing. Among these was the famous Spongeband bowls, which were a part of a whole line of items named Spongeband. The name came from the way they were decorated with a simple band of orange on the tops and sometimes bottom of the pieces. The Spongeband stoneware is very popular and commands a very high price.

Red Wing Spongeware Panel Bowl. 9", no marking, blue/reddish brown, Spongeware paned bowl, $80.00 – 125.00. The bowls were never marked but they are easy to identify as Red Wing. Often they are found with advertising on the inside of the bowl. These advertising bowls are more expensive. The 10" and 11" size without advertising are also more expensive. The 5" bowl is rare to find and commands quite a high price.

RED WING GREEK KEY BOWL. 7", blue/gray, advertising Greek Key bowl, $75.00 – 125.00. Notice the advertising in the center of the bowl pictured below. This was a very popular way for merchants to advertise in early 1900s. Red Wing offered advertising on most of the items they produced. There are collectors who purchase only advertising pieces which are harder to find and make a very interesting collection.

Sewer Pipe

The sewer pipe industry which began in 1891 had a major and long-lasting effect on Red Wing. Owned and operated by Red Wing Stoneware Co., the pipe company carried their name, Red Wing Sewer Pipe Co.

John H. Rich, who was the president of Red Wing Stoneware Co., managed the pipe works and turned his sole attention to it in 1882. A second plant was built bearing his name, the John H. Rich Sewer Pipe Works.

These firms were able to use a lower quality of clay with an overlay of fine stoneware grade and were very successful. The industry continued in Red Wing until the 1970s.

The company made miniature souvenir pieces of the sewer pipe, all with the company name on them. The pieces with "John H. Rich Sewer Pipe Works" are early and rare. There were several varieties with the Red Wing logo on them. The souvenir piece below is one of them.

SEWER PIPE SOUVENIR. 3", face marked "Red Wing Sewer Pipe Corp, Red Wing Minn," $40.00 – 50.00. Some of the pieces were made from the actual pipe clay. These pieces command considerably more money. The later smaller pieces such as this one, had a disk insert with a hole in it to be used as an ashtray.

The stoneware line of Red Wing was discontinued in 1947 and the company concentrated on the art pottery lines. However, the stoneware of Red Wing Stoneware Company holds a special place in history and is one of the most sought after of early collectibles.

A Look at Red Wing Dinnerware

Dinnerware

The dinnerware line of Red Wing Potteries was introduced in the mid 1930s with the Gypsy Trail Line. This line consisted of several patterns, as did all the dinnerware lines. Patterns included Chevron, Reed, Plain, and Fondoso. Charles Murphy, a designer from Ohio, was hired in 1940 to design dinnerware and art pottery. He created patterns with hand-painted designs for the Provincial Line, introduced in 1941. These included Normandy, Orleans, Brittany, and Ardennes. They were some of the most ornate and beautiful of all the patterns. Eva Zeisel, a designer who had been with Red Wing for some years, created the Town & Country Line in 1946.

All the dinnerware consisted of a full line of items including casseroles, coffee and water servers, teapots, salt and pepper shakers, and many serving pieces. The lines were done in a variety of different patterns and colors ranging from solid colors to hand-painted flowers, fruits, and other items. There were many different lines and patterns produced over the years, some in more limited quantities than others. Patterns ranged from quite simple to quite ornate, requiring many brush strokes.

The dinnerware line of Red Wing Potteries was produced until the close of the plant in 1967. A huge seller, the dinnerware line made a large place for Red Wing in the history of such ware. The following examples are just some of the many lines and patterns produced over the years.

PLAIN PATTERN

This pattern is part of the Gypsy Trail Line which also included the Chevron, Reed, and Fondoso patterns. The Plain pattern was produced in 1935, and was the first of the dinnerware. The Plain was produced in a gloss glaze in solid colors of orange, royal blue, yellow, turquoise, and ivory. The pieces could be purchased in a different color of each item.

It included a full line of dinnerware and many accessories such as a cookie jar, beverage servers, and ashtrays. Since this is one of the early dinnerware lines, these pieces are hard to find.

PLAIN SWIRL PITCHER. Orange 64-oz., bottom marked "Red Wing," swirl pitcher, $24.00 – 30.00. This was one of two pitchers in this pattern. The other was a jug type with ice stop.

PLAIN CREAMER & SUGAR. Turquoise and pink 2", bottom marked "Red Wing," $20.00 – 28.00 for both. Notice these pieces are quite small. They almost have the look of miniatures. There was a mustard holder that looked like the sugar bowl except it had a lid.

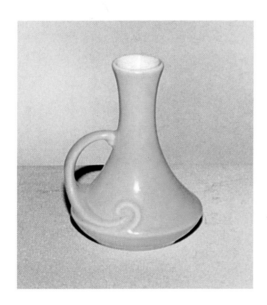

PLAIN OIL CRUET. Yellow 4", bottom marked "Red Wing," oil cruet, $22.00 – 28.00. With the same small swirl as the creamer and sugar these small pieces were a set along with the mustard holder.

PLAIN SALT & PEPPER. Turquoise, 3", no bottom mark, $18.00 – 22.00 set. Notice that these look like miniature teapots. None of the salt and pepper shakers in the Red Wing dinner lines were marked. You will eventually know them by sight.

PROVINCIAL OOMPH

Provincial Oomph was introduced in 1943. The line was a heavy utilitarian dinnerware made in a combination of brown and aqua. This line was produced in a full line of dinnerware and also extensive pieces of bakeware.

PROVINCIAL OOMPH PITCHER. Brown/aqua 60-oz., bottom marked "Red Wing USA," $18.00 – 24.00. Notice that this heavy look resembles the earlier stoneware.

SALAD SETS

Produced in the 1940s these sets contained a 13" bowl and four 8½" plates. The bowl and plates have ribbed edges and are each decorated with a different fruit on a white background. There was a pear, cherries, an apple, and grapes. The bowl was decorated with one of each fruit. Hand painted and very eye catching in bright colors, these sets must have been used at many luncheons in their day.

These salad sets are not often found. A plate may be found occasionally or the bowl. If found as a set it would be quite rare and very expensive. As you can see by the following picture, it was a beautiful set.

SALAD SET PLATE. Yellow pear 8½", bottom marked "Red Wing Pottery Hand Painted," $38.00 – 46.00 each.

PLUM BLOSSOM PATTERN

Plum Blossom was the the only pattern in the Dynasty Line of 1949. A full line of dinnerware, this pattern came in pink and yellow on a white background. The accessories had metallic brown, chartreuse, or forest green exteriors. This pattern, like most of the Red Wing dinnerware, was hand painted and quite attractive.

PLUM BLOSSOM PLACE SETTING. Bottom marked "Red Wing Hand Painted," pink and brown flowers and stems, dinner plate, 10½", $12.00 – 16.00; sauce dish, $7.00 – 10.00; cup, $7.00 – 10.00; saucer, $5.00 – 8.00. Notice the forest green on the inside of the cup, one of the accessory colors.

CHRYSANTHEMUM PATTERN

Part of the Concord Line introduced in 1947, the Chrysanthemum pattern was often referred to as Mum. Produced with hand-painted yellow flowers and green leaves on a white background, this was a very pretty pattern. The accessory pieces came in gray or metallic brown. The metallic brown was used as the color for accessories on many of the dinnerware patterns. Therefore, some of the pieces were interchangeable. It is sometimes hard to tell which accessory goes with which pattern.

CHRYSANTHEMUM DINNER PLATE. Yellow flower, 10½", bottom marked "Red Wing Hand Painted," $10.00 – 15.00. Notice the different shape of the plate. The edges are contoured and rounded up.

MAGNOLIA PATTERN

The Magnolia pattern on the Concord Line was one of the most popular patterns. It was produced with a hand-painted magnolia flower done in a gray and yellow combination with green leaves on a white background. It was a full line of dinnerware with accessory pieces in gray, chartreuse, and metallic. The Concord Line had the most patterns of any of the Red Wing dinnerware lines with 18.

MAGNOLIA SALAD BOWL. Yellow and gray magnolia flower, bottom marked "Red Wing Potteries," salad bowl, $10.00 – 15.00. Notice the touches of black in the color combination.

MAGNOLIA SALT & PEPPER. Gray, no bottom mark, two shaped salt & pepper set, $8.00 – 12.00 pair. Notice the unusual style. Many of the dinnerware salt and pepper sets were an unusual design.

ANNIVERSARY SHAPE

Introduced in 1953, this shape received its name because that year was Red Wing's 75th anniversary. The pieces all have a distinguishing basketweave finish. It was produced in a full line of dinnerware, with the accessories offered in several colors. They were interchangeable with the different patterns and colors.

ANNIVERSARY SALAD BOWL. Pink basket weave, 10½", bottom marked "Red Wing," salad server bowl, $18.00 – 26.00. Notice these pieces had a white interior.

ANNIVERSARY INDIVIDUAL SALAD BOWL. Pink basket weave 5½", bottom marked "Red Wing," anniversary salad bowl, $8.00 – 12.00 each. The two bowls on this page were often used as a chip and dip set along with more of the small bowls.

LOTUS PATTERN

Part of the Concord Line, Lotus was introduced in 1952. A full line of dinnerware, Lotus was hand painted with a flower in a combination of gray, dark brown, and green, with highlights of pink on a white background. This pattern had the same color accessories as the Magnolia pattern. It was also a very popular pattern.

LOTUS PLACE SETTING. White and gray flower, bottom marked "Red Wing Hand Painted USA," dinner plate, 10½", $12.00 – 18.00; salad plate, 7", $6.00 – 10.00; cup, $6.00 – 8.00; saucer, $5.00 – 9.00.

BLOSSOM TIME

Also part of the Concord Line, Blossom Time was introduced in 1952. A very elegant looking pattern, Blossom Time had a hand-painted flower of pink with green leaves accented with yellow and dark brown on a white background. The accessories came in green and yellow, which made the dinnerware even more attractive.

Like all the Red Wing dinnerware, this pattern came in a full line. The plates came in a square shape contoured up at the edges. You have probably noticed by now that the dinner ware plates had many shapes, each adding to the unique look of each pattern.

BLOSSOM TIME PLACE SETTING. Pink and yellow flower, bottom marked "Red Wing Hand Painted," dinner plate, 10½", $10.00 – 16.00; cup, $4.00 – 6.00; saucer, $5.00 – 7.00.

VILLAGE GREEN

Introduced in 1953, Village Green was the second most popular line of Red Wing dinnerware. Its sales spanned a decade. This was a complete line including a 2 gallon water cooler. Glazed in brown and aqua, Village Green was a heavy utilitarian dinnerware.

The line is often confused with the earlier Provincial Oomph. Both were heavy and done in brown and aqua. You will be able to tell the difference due to the fact the colors were put in different places and the Village Green has a ribbed finish.

An identical line, Village Brown, was introduced in 1955. The only difference was the Village Brown was glazed in a plain brown color. Produced with the same molds, this pattern had all the same pieces as the Village Green.

The Village Green line can be found quite often. Probably because of its heavy construction, the pieces were not broken as often as some of the other dinnerware. With some searching you could probably find a complete set of this line, unlike some of the other lines and patterns which could take many years to complete a set.

The following pictures are some of the accessory pieces in the Village Green Line.

VILLAGE GREEN PITCHER. Brown and aqua 10-cup, bottom marked "Red Wing USA," $18.00 – 24.00. There was also a 4-cup pitcher identical to this one.

VILLAGE GREEN BEVERAGE SERVER. Brown and aqua 8-cup with lid, bottom marked "Red Wing USA," $18.00 – 26.00. This pricing assumes that the lid is not cracked or chipped.

VILLAGE GREEN TEAPOT. Brown and aqua 6-cup with lid, bottom marked "Red Wing USA," $18.00 – 26.00. Notice the lighter brown and darker aqua colors. This is probably a newer vintage.

VILLAGE GREEN BEVERAGE MUG, SUGAR BOWL, SYRUP JUG. Brown and aqua, bottom marked "Red Wing USA," Mug, $8.00 – 12.00; sugar bowl, $6.00 – 10.00; syrup jug, $8.00 – 12.00. Notice that the chip in the sugar bowl lid has been glazed over. Undoubtedly done in production you will find this sometimes even on the art pottery.

BOB WHITE

Bob White, the most popular of the dinnerware patterns, was produced from 1956 until the pottery closed in 1967. It was produced in a complete line including a water cooler and a cookie jar. A hand-painted bob white and chicks are rendered in brown and turquoise on a tan flecked background with accents in a darker tan.

Part of the Casual Line along with Smart Set, Tip Toe, Hearthside, and Round Up, the Bob White pattern was quite unique. The salt and pepper shakers were birds along with a larger bird hors d'oeuvre holder. This produced a very attractive and different style dinnerware set.

Most probably in the hands of collectors, this pattern is not easily found. You will see the place settings occasionally but very seldom the accessory pieces. They also command higher prices than the rest of the dinnerware.

BOB WHITE PLACE SETTING. Brown and turquoise, bottom marked "Red Wing USA, Hand Painted, Ovenproof, Detergent Proof," dinner plate, 11", $18.00 – 26.00; cup, $8.00 – 12.00; saucer, $6.00 – 10.00. You will find that most of the dinnerware is sold as separate pieces. Occasionally you will find a place setting or cup and saucer sold together.

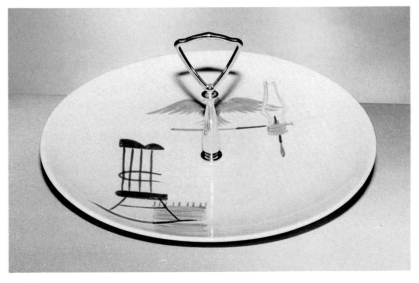

HEARTHSIDE

Introduced in 1961 Hearthside was the last of the Casual Line. This dinnerware was produced with brown, orange, and turquoise pictures on a light tan fleck background. The pictures give the image of a fireplace setting with a home and country motif. There was also a full line of dinnerware.

HEARTHSIDE RELISH TRAY. Brown, turquoise and orange, bottom marked "Red Wing, Hand Painted, Ovenproof, USA," $15.00 – 22.00.

RANDOM HARVEST

Part of the Futura Line, Random Harvest was produced in 1961. It was a full line hand painted in browns, pink, and turquoise on a light tan flecked background. There were numerous leaves and flowers on each piece which required many brush strokes. Random Harvest was advertised as exceptionally well designed and appealing.

Red Wing advertised their dinnerware as hand painted with a freedom of color and a hand-fashioned appearance that establishes fine quality. Their dinnerware did indeed have the look of

fine quality. Red Wing dinnerware sold from $9.00 to $18.00 for a starter set of four place settings, and up to $6.50 per place setting of Bob White. This seems like quite a lot of money for the times. However, considering they were all hand painted, the pricing would have been proportional to hand-painted items in today's dollars.

RANDOM HARVEST RELISH TRAY. Browns, pink, and turquoise, 10½", bottom marked "Red Wing, Hand Painted, Ovenproof, USA," $15.00 – 22.00.

POMPEII

Pompeii was a pattern of the Cylinder or New Shape as it was called. Introduced in 1962 the line was never given a name. A full line of dinnerware produced in browns and turquoise, quite simple but elegant.

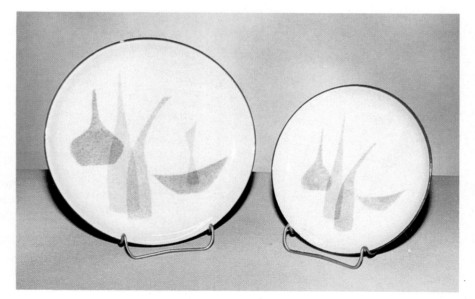

POMPEII SALAD & BB PLATES. Browns and turquoise, no bottom marks, salad plate, $5.00 – 8.00; bread & butter plate, $4.00 – 6.00.

PROVINCIAL

The Provincial was first introduced during World War II as a bakeware line. Reintroduced in 1963 with a full line of dinnerware to match, Provincial is another utilitarian line. The accessories were produced with a tan stone-like finish and bittersweet red interior finish and lids. The plates and other dinnerware items were made in the bittersweet red glaze.

PROVINCIAL BEAN POT. Tan stone 5-quart, bottom marked "Red Wing," $22.00 – 28.00 with lid. This pot originally came with a bittersweet red lid like the following picture.

PROVINCIAL BEAN POT. Tan stone/bittersweet red lid, bottom marked "Red Wing," $16.00 – 22.00.

GREENWICHSTONE & HEARTHSTONE

Both of these patterns were part of the Ceramastone Line introduced in 1967. They were among the last patterns of Red Wing dinnerware produced. The Greenwichstone glazed and hand painted in green and yellow fleck had a swirls in the center which gave the look of being hand turned. The Hearthstone was produced in an orange fleck glaze. These lines did not have the extensive number of pieces of the earlier lines.

GREENWICHSTONE PLATES AND SAUCE DISH. Slate green and yellow fleck, bottom marked "Red Wing, Hand Painted, Ovenproof, USA," dinner plate, 10", $6.00 – 10.00; bread & butter plate, $4.00 – 6.00; sauce dish, $4.00 – 6.00. Notice the brighter yellow fleck on the bottom of the pieces.

HEARTHSTONE PLATE & SAUCE DISH. Orange fleck, bottom marked "Red Wing," dinner plate, 10", $5.00 – 8.00; sauce dish, $3.00 – 6.00. The Hearthstone was also produced in a beige color and was originally made for sale through Sears stores.

Cookie Jars

Red Wing produced several styles of cookie jars. Some were made with a dinnerware pattern, such as Bob White, Round Up, and Happy. Other had a look of their own. There were fruit shapes, drums, pumpkin shape, and a chief jar. Very popular with collectors, they are hard to find in good condition and command quite a high price.

CHIEF COOKIE JAR. Yellow with brown accents, unusual double bottom marked, stamped "Red Wing Pottery Hand Painted," also hand inscribed under glaze "Red Wing USA," $75.00 – 120.00 in very good condition. The hand inscription is identical to some of the art pottery markings.

MISCELLANEOUS PITCHER

MISCELLANEOUS PITCHER. Turquoise, unusual bottom mark reads "Red Wing Potteries Inc. Design Pat. Pending," $24.00 – 32.00. Not known to be part of any line, this pitcher was perhaps a prototype.

Ashtray

The wing ashtray produced by Red Wing was a very popular item. It was used by many companies to advertise. Shaped like the unmistakable red wing that was the pottery's trademark it also was good advertising for Red Wing. Produced mostly in a heavy red glaze, you may occasionally happen upon another color which would be considered quite a find. These ashtrays are popular with collectors. Associated with the rare advertising and miniature pieces, they are a good find.

RED WING ASHTRAY. Top view red glaze, white bottom marked "Red Wing Potteries USA," $40.00 – 55.00. Red Wing also made this ashtray with their 75th anniversary logo on the bottom. Bottom view below.

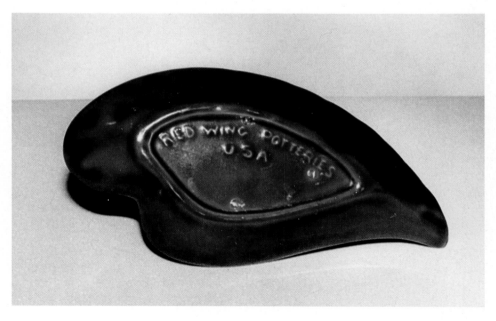

Trivets

Red Wing produced trivets in many of their dinnerware patterns. The also made some for advertising purposes. The following trivet was a special Minnesota Centennial production. Marking the 100th anniversary of Minnesota, the trivet had quite a lot of detail. The bottom marking included a map of the United States with Red Wing, Minnesota, inscribed in a larger scale size in the state of Minnesota.

Other states and companies also purchased trivets with their advertising on them. You will find these pieces made in many different colors and markings.

TRIVET. Top view red, white, bottom marked "Red Wing Potteries, Red Wing Minnesota," and a map of Minnesota, $22.00 – 30.00. A very attractive piece done the heavy red glaze. Bottom view below.

Dinnerware Bottom Markings

There were many different bottom markings used on the Red Wing dinnerware. The following are examples of some of these markings.

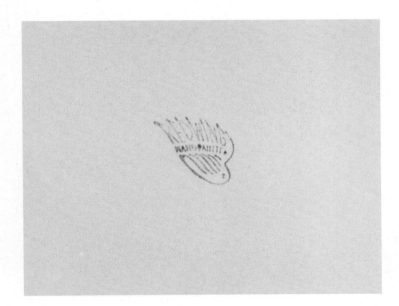

LARGE RED WING & LARGE BLUE WING. Both made with the traditional wing stamp.

INITIAL & LOGO BOTTOM MARKINGS.
Small delicate Red Wing initials
with "Red Wing Pottery Hand Painted," circled around the initials.
Logo marking giving all special
qualities of the dinnerware.

In Closing

Art pottery by definition is any article created by a gifted artist, for beauty rather than utility, and could encompass even tableware.

Few potteries in the United States today are actively creating so-called art pottery. Hand-decorated ware is no longer economically feasible. However, there are some hand-thrown sculptured and decorated wares being produced presently. These few excellent pieces are produced in very limited quantities, a situation that strengthens the importance of art pottery in American history.

There is a Society of Red Wing Collectors that keeps the stoneware and pottery of yesteryear alive. They hold an annual convention in Red Wing, Minnesota, each year. They offer a commemorative piece every year for sale to their members to commemorate Red Wing stoneware and pottery. The pieces are available only to members of the society.

This year, 1995, the commemorative piece was a miniature replica of a novelty planter designed by Charles Murphy. He was very proud of his original, and I am sure would have been equally as proud that one of his pieces was chosen to a souvenir for the society. The following is a picture of that commemorative piece, a fitting tribute to Red Wing art pottery.

COMMEMORATIVE GIRAFFE. 7" **tan/brown flecks, bottom marked, "Red Wing Collectors Society, July 6-8, M-1995, Convention." The original 11" brown with tan flecks, bottom marked #896.**

COLLECTOR BOOKS

Informing Today's Collector

For over two decades we have been keeping collectors informed on trends and values in all fields of antiques and collectibles.

DOLLS, FIGURES & TEDDY BEARS

4707	A Decade of **Barbie** Dolls & Collectibles, 1981–1991, Summers	$19.95
4631	**Barbie** Doll Boom, 1986–1995, Augustyniak	$18.95
2079	**Barbie** Doll Fashions, Volume I, Eames	$24.95
3957	**Barbie** Exclusives, Rana	$18.95
4632	**Barbie** Exclusives, Book II, Rana	$18.95
4557	**Barbie**, The First 30 Years, Deutsch	$24.95
4657	**Barbie** Years, 1959–1995, Olds	$16.95
3310	**Black Dolls**, 1820–1991, Perkins	$17.95
3873	**Black Dolls**, Book II, Perkins	$17.95
1529	Collector's Encyclopedia of **Barbie** Dolls, DeWein	$19.95
4506	Collector's Guide to **Dolls in Uniform**, Bourgeois	$18.95
3727	Collector's Guide to **Ideal Dolls**, Izen	$18.95
3728	Collector's Guide to Miniature **Teddy Bears**, Powell	$17.95
3967	Collector's Guide to **Trolls**, Peterson	$19.95
4571	**Liddle Kiddles**, Identification & Value Guide, Langford	$18.95
4645	**Madame Alexander** Dolls Price Guide #21, Smith	$9.95
3733	**Modern Collector's** Dolls, Sixth Series, Smith	$24.95
3991	**Modern Collector's** Dolls, Seventh Series, Smith	$24.95
4647	**Modern Collector's** Dolls, Eighth Series, Smith	$24.95
4640	Patricia Smith's **Doll Values**, Antique to Modern, 12th Edition	$12.95
3826	Story of **Barbie**, Westenhouser	$19.95
1513	**Teddy Bears & Steiff** Animals, Mandel	$9.95
1817	**Teddy Bears & Steiff** Animals, 2nd Series, Mandel	$19.95
2084	**Teddy Bears, Annalee's & Steiff** Animals, 3rd Series, Mandel	$19.95
1808	Wonder of **Barbie**, Manos	$9.95
1430	World of **Barbie** Dolls, Manos	$9.95

FURNITURE

1457	American **Oak** Furniture, McNerney	$9.95
3716	American **Oak** Furniture, Book II, McNerney	$12.95
1118	Antique **Oak** Furniture, Hill	$7.95
2132	Collector's Encyclopedia of **American** Furniture, Vol. I, Swedberg	$24.95
2271	Collector's Encyclopedia of **American** Furniture, Vol. II, Swedberg	$24.95
3720	Collector's Encyclopedia of **American** Furniture, Vol. III, Swedberg	$24.95
3878	Collector's Guide to **Oak** Furniture, George	$12.95
1755	Furniture of the **Depression Era**, Swedberg	$19.95
3906	**Heywood-Wakefield** Modern Furniture, Rouland	$18.95
1885	**Victorian** Furniture, Our American Heritage, McNerney	$9.95
3829	**Victorian** Furniture, Our American Heritage, Book II, McNerney	$9.95
3869	**Victorian** Furniture books, 2 volume set, McNerney	$19.90

JEWELRY, HATPINS, WATCHES & PURSES

1712	Antique & Collector's **Thimbles** & Accessories, Mathis	$19.95
1748	Antique **Purses**, Revised Second Ed., Holiner	$19.95
1278	Art Nouveau & Art Deco **Jewelry**, Baker	$9.95
4558	**Christmas Pins**, Past and Present, Gallina	$18.95
3875	Collecting Antique **Stickpins**, Kerins	$16.95
3722	Collector's Ency. of **Compacts, Carryalls & Face Powder Boxes**, Mueller	$24.95
4655	Complete Price Guide to **Watches** #16, Shugart	$26.95
1716	Fifty Years of Collectible **Fashion Jewelry**, 1925-1975, Baker	$19.95
1424	**Hatpins** & Hatpin Holders, Baker	$9.95
4570	Ladies' **Compacts**, Gerson	$24.95
1181	100 Years of Collectible **Jewelry**, 1850-1950, Baker	$9.95
2348	20th Century Fashionable Plastic **Jewelry**, Baker	$19.95
3830	Vintage **Vanity Bags & Purses**, Gerson	$24.95

TOYS, MARBLES & CHRISTMAS COLLECTIBLES

3427	**Advertising Character** Collectibles, Dotz	$17.95
2333	Antique & Collector's **Marbles**, 3rd Ed., Grist	$9.95
3827	Antique & Collector's **Toys**, 1870–1950, Longest	$24.95
3956	Baby Boomer **Games**, Identification & Value Guide, Polizzi	$24.95
3717	**Christmas** Collectibles, 2nd Edition, Whitmyer	$24.95
1752	**Christmas** Ornaments, Lights & Decorations, Johnson	$19.95
4649	Classic Plastic **Model Kits**, Polizzi	$24.95

4559	Collectible **Action Figures**, 2nd Ed., Manos	$17.95
3874	Collectible Coca-Cola Toy **Trucks**, deCourtivron	$24.95
2338	Collector's Encyclopedia of **Disneyana**, Longest, Stern	$24.95
4639	Collector's Guide to **Diecast Toys & Scale Models**, Johnson	$19.95
4651	Collector's Guide to **Tinker Toys**, Strange	$18.95
4566	Collector's Guide to **Tootsietoys**, 2nd Ed., Richter	$19.95
3436	Grist's Big Book of **Marbles**	$19.95
3970	Grist's Machine-Made & Contemporary **Marbles**, 2nd Ed.	$9.95
4569	**Howdy Doody**, Collector's Reference and Trivia Guide, Koch	$16.95
4723	**Matchbox®** Toys, 1948 to 1993, Johnson, 2nd Ed.	$18.95
3823	**Mego** Toys, An Illustrated Value Guide, Chrouch	15.95
1540	**Modern Toys** 1930–1980, Baker	$19.95
3888	**Motorcycle** Toys, Antique & Contemporary, Gentry/Downs	$18.95
4728	Schroeder's Collectible **Toys**, Antique to Modern Price Guide, 3rd Ed.	$17.95
1886	Stern's Guide to **Disney** Collectibles	$14.95
2139	Stern's Guide to **Disney** Collectibles, 2nd Series	$14.95
3975	Stern's Guide to **Disney** Collectibles, 3rd Series	$18.95
2028	**Toys**, Antique & Collectible, Longest	$14.95
3979	**Zany Characters** of the Ad World, Lamphier	$16.95

INDIANS, GUNS, KNIVES, TOOLS, PRIMITIVES

1868	Antique **Tools**, Our American Heritage, McNerney	$9.95
2015	Archaic **Indian** Points & Knives, Edler	$14.95
1426	**Arrowheads** & Projectile Points, Hothem	$7.95
4633	**Big Little Books**, Jacobs	$18.95
2279	**Indian** Artifacts of the Midwest, Hothem	$14.95
3885	**Indian** Artifacts of the Midwest, Book II, Hothem	$16.95
1964	**Indian** Axes & Related Stone Artifacts, Hothem	$14.95
2023	**Keen Kutter** Collectibles, Heuring	$14.95
4724	Modern **Guns**, Identification & Values, 11th Ed., Quertermous	$12.95
4505	Standard Guide to **Razors**, Ritchie & Stewart	$9.95
4730	Standard **Knife** Collector's Guide, 3rd Ed., Ritchie & Stewart	$12.95

PAPER COLLECTIBLES & BOOKS

4633	**Big Little Books**, Jacobs	$18.95
1441	Collector's Guide to **Post Cards**, Wood	$9.95
2081	Guide to Collecting **Cookbooks**, Allen	$14.95
4648	Huxford's **Old Book** Value Guide, 8th Ed.	$19.95
2080	Price Guide to **Cookbooks & Recipe Leaflets**, Dickinson	$9.95
2346	**Sheet Music** Reference & Price Guide, 2nd Ed., Pafik & Guiheen	$18.95
4654	**Victorian Trading Cards**, Historical Reference & Value Guide, Cheadle	$19.95

GLASSWARE

1006	**Cambridge Glass** Reprint 1930–1934	$14.95
1007	**Cambridge Glass** Reprint 1949–1953	$14.95
4561	Collectible **Drinking Glasses**, Chase & Kelly	$17.95
4642	Collectible **Glass Shoes**, Wheatley	$19.95
4553	Coll. **Glassware** from the 40's, 50's & 60's, 3rd Ed., Florence	$19.95
2352	Collector's Encyclopedia of **Akro Agate Glassware**, Florence	$14.95
1810	Collector's Encyclopedia of **American Art Glass**, Shuman	$29.95
3312	Collector's Encyclopedia of **Children's Dishes**, Whitmyer	$19.95
4552	Collector's Encyclopedia of **Depression Glass**, 12th Ed., Florence	$19.95
1664	Collector's Encyclopedia of **Heisey Glass**, 1925–1938, Bredehoft	$24.95
3905	Collector's Encyclopedia of **Milk Glass**, Newbound	$24.95
1523	Colors In **Cambridge Glass**, National Cambridge Society	$19.95
4564	**Crackle Glass**, Weitman	$19.95
2275	**Czechoslovakian Glass** and Collectibles, Barta/Rose	$16.95
4714	**Czechoslovakian Glass** and Collectibles, Book II, Barta/Rose	$16.95
4716	**Elegant Glassware** of the Depression Era, 7th Ed., Florence	$19.95
1380	Encyclopedia of **Pattern Glass**, McClain	$12.95
3981	Ever's Standard **Cut Glass** Value Guide	$12.95
4659	**Fenton** Art Glass, 1907–1939, Whitmyer	$24.95
3725	**Fostoria**, Pressed, Blown & Hand Molded Shapes, Kerr	$24.95
3883	**Fostoria Stemware**, The Crystal for America, Long & Seate	$24.95
3318	**Glass Animals** of the Depression Era, Garmon & Spencer	$19.95
4644	**Imperial Carnival Glass**, Burns	$18.95

COLLECTOR BOOKS
Informing Today's Collector

3886 **Kitchen Glassware** of the Depression Years, 5th Ed., Florence \$19.95
2394 **Oil Lamps II**, Glass Kerosene Lamps, Thuro......\$24.95
4725 Pocket Guide to **Depression Glass**, 10th Ed., Florence \$9.95
4634 Standard Encyclopedia of **Carnival Glass**, 5th Ed., Edwards \$24.95
4635 Standard **Carnival Glass** Price Guide, 10th Ed. \$9.95
3974 Standard Encyclopedia of **Opalescent Glass**, Edwards...........\$19.95
4731 **Stemware Identification**, Featuring Cordials with Values, Florence............\$24.95
3326 **Very Rare Glassware** of the Depression Years, 3rd Series, Florence....\$24.95
3909 **Very Rare Glassware** of the Depression Years, 4th Series, Florence..........\$24.95
4732 **Very Rare Glassware** of the Depression Years, 5th Series, Florence..........\$24.95
4656 **Westmoreland Glass**, Wilson \$24.95
2224 World of **Salt Shakers**, 2nd Ed., Lechner.................\$24.95

POTTERY

4630 **American Limoges**, Limoges........................\$24.95
1312 **Blue & White Stoneware**, McNerney \$9.95
1958 So. Potteries **Blue Ridge Dinnerware**, 3rd Ed., Newbound.......\$14.95
1959 **Blue Willow**, 2nd Ed., Gaston....................\$14.95
3816 Collectible **Vernon Kilns**, Nelson.................\$24.95
3311 Collecting **Yellow Ware** – Id. & Value Guide, McAllister \$16.95
1373 Collector's Encyclopedia of **American Dinnerware**, Cunningham \$24.95
3815 Collector's Encyclopedia of **Blue Ridge Dinnerware**, Newbound.....\$19.95
4658 Collector's Encyclopedia of **Brush-McCoy Pottery**, Huxford.........\$24.95
2272 Collector's Encyclopedia of **California Pottery**, Chipman \$24.95
3811 Collector's Encyclopedia of **Colorado Pottery**, Carlton..............\$24.95
2133 Collector's Encyclopedia of **Cookie Jars**, Roerig......\$24.95
3723 Collector's Encyclopedia of **Cookie Jars**, Volume II, Roerig.......\$24.95
3429 Collector's Encyclopedia of **Cowan Pottery**, Saloff..............\$24.95
4638 Collector's Encyclopedia of **Dakota Potteries**, Dommel..........\$24.95
2209 Collector's Encyclopedia of **Fiesta**, 7th Ed., Huxford.....\$19.95
4718 Collector's Encyclopedia of **Figural Planters & Vases**, Newbound \$19.95
3961 Collector's Encyclopedia of **Early Noritake**, Alden...........\$24.95
1439 Collector's Encyclopedia of **Flow Blue China**, Gaston...........\$19.95
3812 Collector's Encyclopedia of **Flow Blue China**, 2nd Ed., Gaston...........\$24.95
3813 Collector's Encyclopedia of **Hall China**, 2nd Ed., Whitmyer.....\$24.95
3431 Collector's Encyclopedia of **Homer Laughlin China**, Jasper.............\$24.95
1276 Collector's Encyclopedia of **Hull Pottery**, Roberts.............\$19.95
4573 Collector's Encyclopedia of **Knowles, Taylor & Knowles**, Gaston \$24.95
3962 Collector's Encyclopedia of **Lefton China**, DeLozier \$19.95
2210 Collector's Encyclopedia of **Limoges Porcelain**, 2nd Ed., Gaston.......\$24.95
2334 Collector's Encyclopedia of **Majolica Pottery**, Katz-Marks.........\$19.95
1358 Collector's Encyclopedia of **McCoy Pottery**, Huxford \$19.95
3963 Collector's Encyclopedia of **Metlox Potteries**, Gibbs Jr. \$24.95
3313 Collector's Encyclopedia of **Niloak**, Gifford \$19.95
3837 Collector's Encyclopedia of **Nippon Porcelain I**, Van Patten \$24.95
2089 Collector's Ency. of **Nippon Porcelain**, 2nd Series, Van Patten \$24.95
1665 Collector's Ency. of **Nippon Porcelain**, 3rd Series, Van Patten \$24.95
3836 **Nippon Porcelain** Price Guide, Van Patten.........\$9.95
1447 Collector's Encyclopedia of **Noritake**, Van Patten \$19.95
3432 Collector's Encyclopedia of **Noritake**, 2nd Series, Van Patten \$24.95
1037 Collector's Encyclopedia of **Occupied Japan**, Vol. I, Florence \$14.95
1038 Collector's Encyclopedia of **Occupied Japan**, Vol. II, Florence \$14.95
2088 Collector's Encyclopedia of **Occupied Japan**, Vol. III, Florence \$14.95
2019 Collector's Encyclopedia of **Occupied Japan**, Vol. IV, Florence \$14.95
2335 Collector's Encyclopedia of **Occupied Japan**, Vol. V, Florence \$14.95
3964 Collector's Encyclopedia of **Pickard China**, Reed..........\$24.95
1311 Collector's Encyclopedia of **R.S. Prussia**, 1st Series, Gaston............\$24.95
1715 Collector's Encyclopedia of **R.S. Prussia**, 2nd Series, Gaston...........\$24.95
3726 Collector's Encyclopedia of **R.S. Prussia**, 3rd Series, Gaston...........\$24.95
3877 Collector's Encyclopedia of **R.S. Prussia**, 4th Series, Gaston...........\$24.95
1034 Collector's Encyclopedia of **Roseville Pottery**, Huxford \$19.95
1035 Collector's Encyclopedia of **Roseville Pottery**, 2nd Ed., Huxford........\$19.95
3357 **Roseville** Price Guide No. 10.................\$9.95
3965 Collector's Encyclopedia of **Sascha Brastoff**, Conti, Bethany & Seay..........\$24.95
3314 Collector's Encyclopedia of **Van Briggle** Art Pottery, Sasicki..........\$24.95
4563 Collector's Encyclopedia of **Wall Pockets**, Newbound \$19.95
2111 Collector's Encyclopedia of **Weller Pottery**, Huxford \$29.95
3452 Coll. Guide to **Country Stoneware & Pottery**, Raycraft...........\$11.95
2077 Coll. Guide to **Country Stoneware & Pottery**, 2nd Series, Raycraft...........\$14.95
3434 Coll. Guide to **Hull Pottery**, The Dinnerware Line, Gick-Burke.........\$16.95

3876 Collector's Guide to **Lu-Ray Pastels**, Meehan \$18.95
3814 Collector's Guide to **Made in Japan** Ceramics, White \$18.95
4646 Collector's Guide to **Made in Japan** Ceramics, Book II, White \$18.95
4565 Collector's Guide to **Rockingham**, The Enduring Ware, Brewer \$14.95
2339 Collector's Guide to **Shawnee Pottery**, Vanderbilt.............\$19.95
1425 **Cookie Jars**, Westfall.......................\$9.95
3440 **Cookie Jars**, Book II, Westfall \$19.95
3435 Debolt's Dictionary of **American Pottery Marks**.................\$17.95
2379 Lehner's Ency. of **U.S. Marks** on Pottery, Porcelain & China \$24.95
4722 **McCoy Pottery**, Collector's Reference & Value Guide, Hanson/Nissen........\$19.95
3825 **Puritan Pottery**, Morris \$24.95
4726 **Red Wing Art Pottery**, 1920s–1960s, Dollen \$19.95
1670 **Red Wing Collectibles**, DePasquale..............\$9.95
1440 **Red Wing Stoneware**, DePasquale...............\$9.95
3738 **Shawnee Pottery**, Mangus....................\$24.95
4629 Turn of the Century **American Dinnerware**, 1880s–1920s, Jasper........\$24.95
4572 **Wall Pockets** of the Past, Perkins...............\$17.95
3327 **Watt Pottery** – Identification & Value Guide, Morris \$19.95

OTHER COLLECTIBLES

4704 Antique & Collectible **Buttons**, Wisniewski \$19.95
2269 Antique **Brass & Copper** Collectibles, Gaston \$16.95
1880 Antique **Iron**, McNerney \$9.95
3872 Antique **Tins**, Dodge........................\$24.95
1714 **Black** Collectibles, Gibbs \$19.95
1128 **Bottle** Pricing Guide, 3rd Ed., Cleveland..........\$7.95
4636 **Celluloid Collectibles**, Dunn \$14.95
3959 **Cereal Box** Bonanza, The 1950's, Bruce \$19.95
3718 Collectible **Aluminum**, Grist...................\$16.95
3445 Collectible **Cats**, An Identification & Value Guide, Fyke \$18.95
4560 Collectible **Cats**, An Identification & Value Guide, Book II, Fyke \$19.95
1634 Collector's Ency. of Figural & Novelty **Salt & Pepper Shakers**, Davern........\$19.95
2020 Collector's Ency. of Figural & Novelty **Salt & Pepper Shakers**, Vol. II, Davern...\$19.95
2018 Collector's Encyclopedia of **Granite Ware**, Greguire \$24.95
3430 Collector's Encyclopedia of **Granite Ware**, Book II, Greguire \$24.95
4705 Collector's Guide to **Antique Radios**, 4th Ed., Bunis..........\$18.95
1916 Collector's Guide to **Art Deco**, Gaston \$14.95
3880 Collector's Guide to **Cigarette Lighters**, Flanagan \$17.95
4637 Collector's Guide to **Cigarette Lighters**, Book II, Flanagan \$17.95
1537 Collector's Guide to **Country Baskets**, Raycraft.........\$9.95
3966 Collector's Guide to **Inkwells**, Identification & Values, Badders \$18.95
3881 Collector's Guide to **Novelty Radios**, Bunis/Breed \$18.95
4652 Collector's Guide to **Transistor Radios**, 2nd Ed., Bunis \$16.95
4653 Collector's Guide to **TV Memorabilia**, 1960s–1970s, Davis/Morgan \$24.95
2276 **Decoys**, Kangas............................\$24.95
1629 **Doorstops**, Identification & Values, Bertoia \$9.95
4567 Figural **Napkin Rings**, Gottschalk & Whitson \$18.95
3968 **Fishing Lure** Collectibles, Murphy/Edmisten..........\$24.95
3817 **Flea Market Trader**, 10th Ed., Huxford \$12.95
3976 Foremost Guide to **Uncle Sam** Collectibles, Czulewicz \$24.95
4641 **Garage Sale & Flea Market Annual**, 4th Ed. \$19.95
3819 **General Store Collectibles**, Wilson \$24.95
4643 **Great American West** Collectibles, Wilson \$24.95
2215 Goldstein's **Coca-Cola** Collectibles...............\$16.95
3884 Huxford's Collectible **Advertising**, 2nd Ed.........\$24.95
2216 **Kitchen Antiques**, 1790–1940, McNerney \$14.95
3321 Ornamental & Figural **Nutcrackers**, Rittenhouse \$16.95
2026 **Railroad** Collectibles, 4th Ed., Baker.............\$14.95
1632 **Salt & Pepper Shakers**, Guarnaccia \$9.95
1888 **Salt & Pepper Shakers** II, Identification & Value Guide, Book II, Guarnaccia ..\$14.95
2220 **Salt & Pepper Shakers** III, Guarnaccia \$14.95
3443 **Salt & Pepper Shakers** IV, Guarnaccia \$18.95
4555 **Schroeder's Antiques Price Guide**, 14th Ed., Huxford \$12.95
2096 **Silverplated Flatware**, Revised 4th Edition, Hagan \$14.95
1922 Standard **Old Bottle** Price Guide, Sellari..........\$14.95
4708 Summers' Guide to **Coca-Cola**..................\$19.95
3892 **Toy & Miniature Sewing Machines**, Thomas \$18.95
3828 Value Guide to **Advertising Memorabilia**, Summers \$18.95
3977 Value Guide to **Gas Station** Memorabilia, Summers & Priddy \$24.95
3444 **Wanted to Buy**, 5th Edition \$9.95

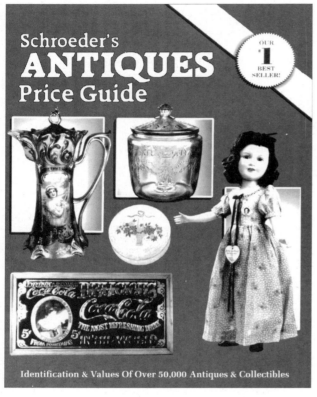